THE MAFIA PRINCIPLE

Joseph Antonio Raffaele
Drexel University

University Press
of America™

Foreword

What ails our society is not an inability on the part of science and technology to find answers to problems. The difficulty lies in the institutional arrangements of countervailing power through which the society's decisions pass. There is a deep mistrust in the land in the government and corporate organizations through which decisions flow.

The modern technological society that has issued from western culture has rendered this traditional decision-making process obsolete. We have a process that generates a clash of obsolete liberal and conservative ideologies pitting self-serving information against each other, whose end result is more state intervention; that recoils from facing up to the facts; that makes choices under intense egalitarian pressures; that cynically seeks to amuse the populace in exchange for profit, power, and prestige for the managers.

An outcome of such ingredients in decision making is a paralysis of effective action. Out of such impairment an equality of mediocrity emerges whose residues are fraudulent relationships and an omnipotent state.

The system of countervailing power used to work reasonably well in coming up with solutions. But now, to arrest the march toward chaos or the omnipotent state, institutional re-arrangements are required. We need in effect what may be difficult to achieve: the subordination of mass organization to the individual, the dissemination of honest information, and the development of a freedom-loving but morally responsible individual.

In short, the underlying problem is moral in character. But works in the social sciences ignore this normative question or relegate it to a final and brief exhortation. An alternative--preachment--generates boredom. Accordingly, I have elected to deliver the message on the political economy of organized advocacies through irreverent exposition. The approach generates heat--and works.

In support of my thesis, I bring forward the following: the characteristics of government and corporate organization, racial and ethnic issues, and the posture of American intellectuals. I do so because of my belief that the factors accounting for the collapse of trust are to be found in these areas.

I want to express my thanks to Joseph Mark Raffaele for his many stimulating philosophical thoughts during the preparation of this work.

Table of Contents

Preface

0758824

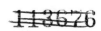

Preface:

    I first began to develop the notion of a mafia principle during my childhood on the Brooklyn waterfront. My father was an immigrant from Sicily. He brought his family into a neighborhood whose bosses were shanty Irishmen with angry faces. Down at the docks one night, an Irish policeman shoved my father against a wall and frisked him. Like inner-city blacks of these days, Gianni was suspect simply because he belonged to an inferior group. He blew his stack. A black jack on the back of his head pacified him. This and other events in those early days etched in my mind the similarities between the legitimate and illegitimate elements in society.

    Those madmen from Ireland not only threatened my father, but they gave me trouble also. A big tough by the name of Ryan was constantly either beating me up or threatening to. I hired Murray Gendell to protect my brittle body. Murray's mother tried to help, too; she kept feeding me matzoh ball soup. Finally I got expelled from parochial school for urinating over the granite slab in the privy onto Ryan's head. It was a remarkable feat, but he ran off complaining to Sister Brennan. She sided with the Irish. Soon thereafter an Italian backlash spread through the area. It became all right in my community to make love to an Irish woman, but to bring one into the family was an act of dishonor.

    My clan was poor, and some members were even predatory. But we all lived by a moral code. We had self-respect; poverty was not an excuse for lack of civility. The contemporary generation of poor, under cover of darkness, loot the homes and stores of the unprotected--even each other; my clan would have considered these looters vulgar, _cafoni_. The people in our neighborhood who were called _mafiosi_ may have been treated like criminals by outsiders, but they provided a service. When they committed violence, it was on each other, not on the innocent. Nor did they commit violence for its own sake. The Sicilians did not loot the dry goods store of the Jews down the street. But the owners of such an establishment would not feel safe today. They are under a state of siege by denizens of those neighborhoods, many of them, by day, customers at the very stores they raid at night. The blacks justify their actions by calling the Jewish shopkeepers interlopers and exploiters. The Jews are closing up shop and fleeing to safer ground. But in the neighborhood where I grew up, there was no ethic of entitlement. What one wanted could only be claimed in return for a service, not by invoking human rights. To my recollection, nobody explained his condition by whining about oppression.

By current sociological standards, Italians suffered from unemployment, inadequate housing, poor diets. But there was no welfare, no desertion of families by fathers, no mugging, no abuse of women. Family and relatives provided the means to cope. Nor were the manifestations of poverty entirely unrewarding. Cockroaches and mice, the bane of my mother's existence, were a fascination to my brothers. Italian bread with a touch of olive oil heated in the coal oven was a fabulous treat. It took only a discarded fruit box, board, and roller skates to fashion a classy scooter. Among the other fascinations of my block were the members of the Anastasia family. They had charisma. The activity in and around their brownstone was exciting. Later, Albert Anastasia, my idol, got shot in a barber's chair. He died of natural causes accelerated by the precipitous entrance of bullets into his body. To outsiders, the activities of the Anastasia family were illegitimate, and Albert Anastasia's end seemed bizarre but fitting.

Yet the intensive competition at the end of the block in Bush terminal across from Governor's Island was considered American and proper. To my family, the relationship there was dog-eat-dog. Gianni had the habit of trying to terminate each social encounter with a sense of good feeling all around. He soon discovered that this goal was not considered good American business. The business ethos clashed with the family ethos in a society permeated by the zest for making a buck. My father learned that in dealings beyond the family everybody expected to be screwed by everybody else. The official distinctions, accordingly, between the legitimate and illegitimate mafia, began to blur.

Unable to speak the evasive language of the legitimate mafia, I enrolled in liberal arts at City College Evening Division. This was before City College began to specialize in the matriculation of functional illiterates. Jobs were scarce and most of them part time: hustler at Ebbetts Field, diver for pilfered goods at the pier, spearsman in the triumphal scene of _Aida_. Then I landed a job as factory hand during the day and numbers runner in the swing shift. When my boss got shot, I quietly switched to the day session.

That was about the time my family began to go places. My mother started to sew straps on bras at thirty cents an hour. I used to count them and fantasize; women seemed to have bigger bosoms in those days. When my sister got a job as a switchboard operator at Bell Telephone, we really began to move up. Gianni would brag about Ciccina working for the telephone cumpanee. Today, by law, the offer of such a job to a black woman may be considered not so much a sign of upward movement for blacks as a sign of white oppression. But Ciccina didn't feel oppressed; she felt like a success, and the family admired her for it.

Later war broke out. With my ability to speak French, Italian, and Sicilian, I was ready to save democracy in Europe; but the Army shipped me to the China-Burma-India theater where they speak Chinese, Burmese, and Hindustani. Promotions came fast--from private to major-- each of my commanders using the management principle of upgrading to unload a problem.

After the war, my Army career fell into crisis. The Department of Defense found me lacking in educational qualifications. The D.O.D. _mafiosi_ would not accept my graduate-level studies in economics as a substitute for the Army's requirement: a correspondence course in basic economics. If their decision stuck, it would mean the loss of lush pension rights and the opportunity for entrance into the racket of double dipping. I wrote a denunciatory letter and then went down to Washington to underscore its message with appropriate gestures.

With the termination of my Army career (and pension rights), I entered civilian society, where the mafia principle really began to bloom. My job as labor boss on the waterfront was illuminating. After I had taught the stevedores and longshoremen how to make deals over the table, the Wasp mayor, to mend his sagging political fortunes, pulled the rug from under me by intervening in a dispute on the side of the longshoremen. Mainstream society was endorsing the very methods that I was urging the men to abandon. I quit after advising the men to take up bird watching.

My childhood patterns of thinking generated perplexity as I entered Wasp circles. What high Wasp society deemed inferior behavior in my group often struck me as superior. Moreover, some of the behavior deemed inferior was not indigenous to Italians, but filtered down from the superior group. Accordingly, while I felt at times like an outsider, there were moments when moving in Wasp circles gave me the feeling of being home again.

Reaching ever higher into more respectable society, I found a job as a college professor. The academic life evoked memories of my boyhood; the university that hired me provided quarters for many flourishing rackets. Professors were using the premises as a hideout for lucrative deals with government and industry. The people in the place--they were referred to as a community of scholars--turned out to be a collection of soloists adept at playing the politics of self-aggrandizement. They referred to themselves as liberals. Taking this liberal atmosphere at face value, I organized a prep school for poor blacks in the neighborhood, but my association ended after a year because the university's president blew his cool and knuckled under to a black _mafioso_. The boss stripped me of épaulettes, sword, and gold buttons.

Observing students at the university who tilted with administrators, I imagined a revision of the fables of La Fontaine: once upon a time, there lived a colony of affluent grasshoppers. The adults spent most of their time examining their way of life in sociology courses and becoming angry with each other over their different points of view. The young grasshoppers, members of Consciousness III, waited for predigested food to be brought to them by their admiring parents. Nobody dared to tell the children how the food was grown; it was not relevant to their experience. The grasshopper psychiatrists warned that such information would damage their development. Down the road a way there was an ant heap whose passages echoed with toil. The ants were too busy to brood over their development. None of them knew there was a self-awareness to develop. One day, the adult grasshoppers, exhausted from predigesting food and affluent living, died from circulatory arrest. The young grasshoppers demanded their human rights to predigested food. And the ants obliged by eating them up.

Puzzlement over these attitudes brought me to the library. I soon discovered that Americans are enthusiastic believers in demons. The idea of a prevalent but obscure conspiracy---whether of war lords, assassins, communists, or crime syndicates---excites people. The conviction that a conspiracy is afoot triggers feelings akin to those that come from reading ghost stories, sensations that provide relief from many afflictions, including difficult menopause. Here I felt I had discovered a clue to the sources of my perplexity.

Three critical ingredients seem to frame a conspiracy: First, the event---almost any event---must be associated with a group of persons whose relationships and purposes are unclear. Second, the behavior of such people must be described as perplexing but nefarious. It helps in such description to use the term "take-over". The take-over may include seizures of nuclear plants, banks, the world oil supply, the solar system. Last, suggest that for arcane reasons the government is engaging in foot-dragging against the conspiracy.

The economy can ill-afford extinction of the most titillating of all intrigues---the mafia conspiracy. Politicians, judges, police officers, writers, and newspapermen would be deprived of their sustenance. Informers would lose the opportunity of telling their employers what their bosses would like to hear. The film industry would be denied the right to make blockbuster profits. In short, a crippling blow would be dealt the gross national product of the economy. Here, in the idea of a mafia conspiracy, I sensed being close to a fundamental principle.

In Sicily, the term "mafia" originally referred to an informal organization protecting people against oppression by the state. In the United
States, the word has come to be used as a synonym for organized crime.
The New York Times suggests that organized crime is under the management
of persons of Italian ancestry. This alone, lumping together Sicilians
with ordinary Italians, is enough to make mafia blood boil. The Times
interprets a complex phenomenon by an obsolete system of thought, and,
characteristic of American liberalism, embellishes a label with a pretense of scholarly analysis.

Enunciating the gospel, Time Magazine describes the mafia as an organization of some five thousand persons of Italian ancestry doing a forty-
eight billion dollar business annually. The dollar figure amounts to the
entire income of many nations. One may marvel at how persons of limited
education can manage such a business. Without degrees in business administration, they perform miracles in management. Time gives no clue to
this mystery, although it does point out that the mafia is moving quietly
into legitimate business. An impartial observer would evaluate the same
pheonomenon deplored by Time as upward mobility into legitimate society.
At the very least, one has to draw the inference from such accounts that
organization of such dimension could not survive without support from the
influential in legitimate society.

According to the same mass media, the mafia is integrating its forces.
They report that a person by the name of Meyer Lansky is a top associate
with blacks as his collectors. A newspaper account ties air freight thefts
with a member of Cosa Nostra by the name of Davidoff. These associations
suggest that the syndicate should be renamed Kosher Nostra. These official
realities also suggest the way toward a more integrated society: amend the
equal opportunity law to require placement of Wasp businessmen into top
posts of the syndicate and Italians so displaced in top positions of corporations.

Niccolo Machiavelli's letter asking Lorenzo de Medici for a job
suggests how a college professor can develop from these facts of American
life a mafia principle. Like Niccolo, he can offer the princes of power
in legitimate society neither horses, cloth of gold, weapons, precious
stones, nor similar ornaments. But he can enlighten them about the differences and similarities between the legitimate and illegitimate mafia.
Through the mafia principle, he can interpret the hidden meaning underlying society's push toward equality.

The mafia principle affirms the tendency in western civilization to
capsulate human activity into ever bigger organization; to replace individual morality with organization morality; to subordinate the individual
to the demands of organization; and in the clash between organizations,
to develop an equality of mediocrity. The mafia principle describes a

dimension of the tendency in western society of increasing evil. Things go from good to bad and from bad to worse. They do so because what is good for the individual is eventually sought in organized fashion, becomes bad for the society as a whole, and, in the long run, for the individual himself. This tendency in social evolution compels a constant examination of legitimacy, so that what appears to be legitimate, upon scrutiny, becomes illegitimate. If we were to look at the history of western civilization in its evolution from simple to complex societies, we would find a process of examining legitimacy by the periodic intervention of government. By such a process, the course of western civilization has been one of develop) g a religion of the state. Under such a religion, the individual loses his individuality and his political life. The system begins to count on the development of a mass man who will not rebel if kept well fed and well amused.

Unhappily, this governmental solution to the escalating effects of greed is no longer a solution. It has brought a system of massive manipulation against which the individual cannot react rationnally. The restraints imposed by a market system have failed. The restraints imposed by government have failed. There are grave doubts that the system, in effect, can develop a process that would cause its extinction.

There used to be different classes managing the various functions in society. Thus, intellectuals--the writers of ideas--were one; politicians providing favors to individuals in exchange for support were another; clergymen dispensing a supportive faith were a third; philanthropists furnishing the financial means for the enjoyment of the arts were a fourth; and a merchant class for the distribution of consumer goods a fifth. Now, if we were to project existing trends into the future, we would find that these functions are coming together under the umbrella of huge corporate conglomerates with the approval of the state. As conglomerates mushroom, they compete less with each other, prefering to act in accordance with the mafia principle of tacitly respecting each other's duchies. As the conglomerates gobble up big corporations, the multiplicity of tongues with which decisions are made diminishes. Moreover, the process is accelerated as government sanctions corporate political action committees which have begun the next stage of removing the individual from the political process. The publication of ideas, the development of science and technology, the enjoyment of art and leisure, the consumption of goods are being increasingly channeled within corporate structures which at their summit are tied to government. Directly and indirectly, through the taxing and spending function of government, the producers, artists, technicians, scientists, university professors, are becoming quasi-public employees managed by corporate executives. Thus, the system's managers emerge as the new managing class whose members shuttle back and forth between umbrella conglomerate and collaborating government. And this managing class is the new mafia.

The mafia principle applies to all the society's institutions. The Peter principle, worthy lineal ancestor and notable breakthrough in modern management theory, affirmed that each of us rises in an organization to our level of incompetence. The mafia principle recognizes the next stage of organization: increasing homogenization in the attitudes of people and in the characteristics of organizations by a process of leveling up and leveling down. The principle applies to all institutions, from the United States Presidency to the numbers racket of the most humble member of the Family. The mafia, you see, is everywhere; in corporate organization, universities, government bureaucracies. Observe, for example, how a small group of mafiosi in the government converted equal opportunity into a nice racket for blacks. Time lag accounts for the differences. The price of organization, any organization, is corruption. And corruption, simply expressed, is the disparity in the evolution of an organization between stated purpose and actual practice.

The mafia is an attitude of mind, a concept of self and one's relationship to institutions and people. As an idea, it is a sense of obligation that vanishes beyond loyalty to one's family. As a practice, the mafia is the employment of conspiratorial organization power to promote self-interest. The mafia principle affirms that the society's members in their pursuit of self-interest abhor differences; through the medium of conspiratorial organization, they narrow them by a process of leveling. The consequence is an equality of mediocrity. The pursuit of organized self-interest turns into a racket at the expense of other groups. The predatory acts of self-interest duchies generate counter-organization. Traditional groups and emerging counter-groups adopt each other's practices. Those in the ascendancy seek equality. Equilibrium is achieved by a state-imposed equality of mediocrity.

In effect, the mafia attitude is not confined to society's criminal elements. The Italian immigrants who have pursued successful criminal careers have had fertile and friendly American soil in which to develop their talents. With the help of liberal thinking, the society's social redemption proceeds through the pursuit of equality that either eliminates differences or makes them a subject of improper discourse. The liberal ethic of making things better leads to solutions whose results require new formulas to remedy the new problems they create. The end of the road is state-supervised equality of mediocrity.

To state the urgency of this message would be to stress the obvious. We need to clarify the forces behind organizational equality in modern life. I therefore recommend this work to corporate executives, public officials, university presidents, directors of feminist organizations, the executives of crime syndicates, and those segments of the public, male and female, who have not succeeded in latching onto a lucrative racket. Through the mafia principle, Italian-Americans offer insight into the meaning of integration in American society.

The mafia principle applies generally to all managers of the system.

University presidents, for example, may appear to be excluded. Their
language is more bland, more qualified, and less controversial than that
of corporate managers. Their distinct competence lies in the ability to
make eloquent statements of little substance. Beneath the surface of language, nevertheless, university presidents operate in the same mafia style.

I cannot help thinking that the mafia principle may seem to be an
appeal to anti-intellectualism. Not so. Rather, it is an exhortation to
undertake a critical examination of liberalism. By the public policy they
espouse, liberals are foremost contributors to the expansion of the mafia
mentality. They claim to represent all mankind, but they have lost touch
with particular kinds of men. They claim to love all humanity, but hold
some groups in contempt. They have converted us into social groups, economic classes, preferred categories, concepts, to the point where we have
difficulty discerning reality. The marriage of Marixism and Liberalism
has boxed us in. On balance, we would be better off had Karl Marx never
existed. Liberalism has become a world of abstraction to the point of
meaninglessness and illusion.

The evolution of liberalism commences with the ferment stirred to redress moral wrong and ends with a society of passionless equality and universal fantasy hiding the mafia reality underneath. To grasp the thread
that traces this moral outcome of western culture, this work begins with
vignettes from the land where the mafia originated, and continues across
the sea in America where mafiaismo triumphs in modern clothes. The account
ends with a fundamental question: does western man beget evil by his organized attempts to correct evil?

PART ONE: Introduction

Chapter 1

The Land of the Mafia

The vignettes that follow are of persons in a Sicilian village.
They transcend local interest. They reveal the sources of Italian-
American attitudes: sanctity of neighborhood; the fraudulent character of relationships beyond the family; mistrust of government; the
dishonor befalling a man who fails to discharge his moral obligations;
the view of food as a symbol of God; the importance of assuming a
position of dignity, absence of which makes one a cafone. But as they
become middle class in the modern cities of Italy, these people begin
to display the gamut of twentieth-century tensions. They become more
complex and more devious. The social bond collapses. And this destruction eventually evolves into a new kind of violence that has
nothing to do with correcting moral wrong. Thus, the vignettes are
a summation of western civilization's course. By attending to them,
we hear ourselves.

Pino is poor and without power or powerful connections. Therefore he is a victim of the powerful in his village. He has a vision
of equality, in which even the smallest decisions are collectively
arrived at, yet he knows that only Christ has the power to equalize.
Pino says:

> They arrested me because I took weeds along the road
> to feed the animals. I do not have any land. So I pass
> along a place and say: would you let me have a handful of
> fodder like this? And they may say no. They were watching
> that day and they grabbed me. They took me into the village
> and threw me in jail; because I was trying to live.

> There is nothing good about Sicilians. Because if
> I have a need and come to you for a few pennies, you say:
> brother, if I do, when would you give them back? I cannot
> possibly give them back. And right there I lose my honor.

> If I were the mayor of this town, I would call all
> the peasants to a meeting and say: it is right to do this.

Tell me, is it right to place this cigarette here or a little more over there? And then someone would say: more toward the center. Then we would come to an agreement and do something.

Do you know what should be done with this poverty? Jesus Christ should make us all equal or dead. And to be equal, one should not have to beg.

In spite of his opinions, Pino recognizes his disenfranchisement from the prerogatives of power. Some of the poor have analyzed their situation and have pinpointed the sources of power. They blame their plight on the mafia. Nino says:

This village is shit. I would go if I had the train fare. The mafia are the ones who get things done here. They know how to settle matters. If a controversy exists, you go to them for a decision. They believe themselves to be persons of great worth. The authorities cannot be taken seriously. If a shot is heard, they do not get close. They have their salary; so why get in a mess?

Salvatore agrees:

The mafia gets things done here. It is not the lawyers certainly. The mafiosi are the interpreters of the village. They settle matters. If a controversy exists you go to them for a decision.

Pina explains how mafia methods affect life-and-death matters in the village. She knows the official record does not give a true account of matters. The villagers understand only too well the difference between reality and the official newspaper version of events.

No. I do not know about these things by reading the papers. I listen to someone say: they killed Tizio for some trivial matter. But who knows what the truth is? When they killed Angeluzzo Marchese they did it by mistake. He was a good guy even if the police had a tab on him. They were aiming at someone else who was a fly on their nose. They said in the village that he was really a bad character. He was a money lender and they shot at him several times. It was right; it was right. But Angeluzzo was with him.

-10-

When something is done to people, such as a slap on the
face, if they do not take away the sting, they cannot rest.
Once a cousin did this to another cousin and he died. Over
nothing. Another time two of the men quarreled over a trifle,
They ended up in blows and then one of them in order to
avenge himself, goes and cuts down the trees of the other.
And there went his patrimony.

Some men are disgruntled with this exercise of raw power. Like Nino,
they envision a system of cooperation. Franco says:

To eliminate the mafia there ought to be a law that
carries matters to an end. Then things would go well.
Since there is no such law, the mafia does as it pleases.

Men should give each other mutual support. They should
not be looking at a man as a grand signore because he has a
few more lire than I do. Or that he should not even look at
me while I, in fact, could be superior to him.

The people have omertà. Omertà is when you keep your
words in your stomach. It is being a real man. It means
a brotherhood of mutual respect. A world without jealousy.

Everybody should be equal. Everyone should be well
placed in a job. Whenever something happens, a man should
have his honor preserved. Then you will see how nice
things could be.

Sure there are young men who would like to be mafiosi.
That way they can impose on people; kick another person
with the point of one's shoe. A friend greets him and he
says: But who has ever seen you before? That is after
he has made a pile of money. And how has he done that?
By scratching, by robbing, by doing bad things. If
there was equality, no one could possibly be a mafioso.

Santo continues this line of thinking, of the notion that with equality
comes a greater purity of spirit. He defines the mafia as a system based
purely on power and self-interest.

What is the mafia? It is when a wife cuckolds a husband
and he draws his knife and kills her. It is when people do
not find work and they go down to the employment office and
say if you do not give me work I will break your head. It
is when the one who has everything does not work.

-11-

Some years ago there was a murder of a rural watchman in the village. He and his colleague were working together in the countryside. One of them was then offered a good position as a policeman of the town. The other was poisoned with envy. There was a villa stocked with fruit which they had to guard. One night they decided to keep a watchful eye. One of them gave it to the other twice. Then, while his victim was twisting and turning on the ground, he gave him another two. Later, someone passed by and he said: "Look, they have killed my colleague." The passerby went down to the police barracks. The other fellow, all in tears, walked to the village shouting how they had killed his colleague.

In the morning there was a police investigation. He kept repeating that it was a shepherd who had done the deed. They arrested all the shepherds. Then there was the funeral and the fellow went along so beautifully you would never have suspected anything. But they brought his gun to Agrigento and concluded he had done it.

Then there was another incident that led to a homicide. A truck driver borrowed some money from a woman. Then, telling her that he was taking her home, he tied her up with a piece of rope and broke her head with a cane. He placed some fennel under her arms. He threw the cane in the garage. But the police found it. He was given a life sentence.

We have a character in the village who scored three homicides. He had been given a medal for killing a bandit. He used to go around with the medal and an automatic pistol. One day he had a quarrel with a policeman and off he went to kill him. He was coming down from the high point of the village when an old woman passed him by on the road. She asked him: "What are you doing?" So he let her have it too in order not to get crossed up.

But most homicides are questions of honor. Someone offends a brother and he has to be avenged. What sort of impression would this make if he does not do so? He is a fool, they would say. Even if he has peaceful sentiments, the voices that rise in the village are enough to make him kill.

Eventually, Santo's anecdotes come to a philosophical acceptance that the mafia principle is based, after all, on human nature, and Luigi agrees:

When I was a boy, I wanted to be a good Christian. But it cannot be because the possibilities do not exist. The rich man is always rich and the poor man is always poor. I have to work with his money. I only have my arms. The rich man always thinks of himself. He is always making accounts; five thousand for rope; a thousand here; another thousand there. The rich grab everything while we go with a hoe tied to our necks.

I wanted to amount to something. But my head is not my own. I was taken off to be a soldier. And then four soldiers hauled me back to the village because I'm supposed to be a madman. For me, success is no longer possible. I would like to become a boy again to understand better what I want.

Those who live well know how to talk; not I who live like a mule. If I do not work I cannot eat. If I work, I can bring a piece of bread to the children. If I do not work, I bring nothing. We eat bread and pasta; two loaves of bread and a half kilo of pasta each day. We cannot buy meat. It would give me indigestion. The rich eat a second course, but we do not.

If I were the mayor of this miserable village and had a hundred million lire, I would give twenty thousand to this one and another twenty thousand to that one. I would give them the means to live. Or else I would give them work. But the mayor doesn't do right. He provides work for the shoemakers and the stone masons but not for the poor.

The rich look after their pocketbooks and don't give a damn about the poor. Crimes occur because of food and drink. I rob you and you recognize me. Pig of hell, I say, he had recognized me. I must shoot him. And I kill in order to eat.

We should all be equal and be able to appear in the midst of other Christians. Only the one who has money knows how to reason.

Nicola complains about the apathy that allows such a system to flourish.

We talk; we discuss; and then at the time of doing battle nobody shows up, not even Jesus Christ. We are timid. We once went on strike against the land tax and forty or so showed up. I have to unload some fertilizer, said one. I have to bring some grain to the mill, said another. I say: take a shit a long way off.

These men complain about inequality. They envision a perfect world of equality. Whatever their complaints or dreams, these people know that if they expect to survive in their culture, they must find and placate the real sources of power in their village. They must be disposed to kiss hands.

These people live in the Sicilian village of Noro, where, after a sleep of centuries, the shock of change produces bizarre results. Juke boxes and pinball machines are transported in donkey carts. A young girl in high heels steps out gingerly from a stone house to avoid the manure. Down the street from the Bar Moderno, a woman scrubs the threshold of her home in a futile attempt to keep the filth at a distance. An automobile with antenna at full mast covers with dust a peasant who travels two hours by mule to reach his piece of land by six in the morning. He shares his single room with the animal. The mule might soil the street; a contravention of the law.

These contrasts bespeak a multitude of events, some planned, but most willy-nilly. The young who migrate to the North of Italy bring money and ideas back to the village. Peasants become dissatisfied with bread and pasta. They compare themselves with the prosperous people of the community and find themselves wanting. Women venture forth alone beyond the cobblestone streets in which they live. Politicians, social idealists, priests woo the new sovereign--the semiliterate person asserting new tastes. The values of mass markets drive out inner-directed traditional values. The new symbol of modernity is a transistor radio held high by a passerby like a votive offering. The new mass man reads comic books, newspapers devoted to sports, and weeklies that keep him informed on the sex habits of celebrities.

It is difficult to single out the persons who hold power in the village. The prominent persons may be puppets. Those who live wisely ferret out the hidden centers of power and pay homage in return for a favor come a rainy day. It is difficult to determine the facts. What people say openly is a Pirandellian convenience of the moment that varies with particular circumstances one has to face.

The mafia becomes intelligible when placed in the context of this obsession with power. A villager defends himself through granting and banking favors. He renders a benefit and banks the reciprocity for use at a future date. Sometimes it does not work, and he falls on his face.

This banking operation is resorted to because organized society cannot be counted upon to dispense justice. The one who suffers a wrong must rely on his own intervention. Unless he takes the initiative against the evil-doer, he may suffer unbearable criticism from the community. To obtain justice, he may have to draw from his account.

This cynicism partly derives from the fact that his perception of reality is not first hand, but is distilled through the intelligence of others. This difficulty he has of determining what is real reinforces his suspicions of society. The only trustworthy relationships are those of the family.

His Roman Catholicism strengthens the same obsession with power. He approaches God as a supplicant for relief from the bestial existence on earth. God (or Christ; he draws no distinction), is a force to be reckoned with. He is exacting at times, and little can be done about it. In contrast, the Virgin Mary and the saints are not symbols of unremitting power but almost human intermediaries who can be appealed to for intercession. God and Mary are the masculine and feminine aspects of religious faith. Those who appeal to feminine intermediaries are more successful. But even so, matters more likely than not are apt to go wrong. One has to expect failure more than success.

The people of Noro wear this pessimism on their faces. They are caught in a closed circle of pessimism. Misfortune reinforces their pessimism and the more virulent pessimism breeds more misfortune. So keep your cards close to your chest and what you feel keep in your stomach. "Cu sulu joca cu nuddu si sciarria." He who plays the game alone does not quarrel with anyone, states the local proverb.

At times, this pessimism erupts into rage. One can easily rub people the wrong way. Innocently developed situations acquire an exaggerated importance. Concessions only result in a loss of dignity. I recall buying a drink at a roadside stand. A man beside me interpreted the acceptance of my order before his as an affront. He slammed a coin on the counter and bellowed: "Quannu parlu io, vogiu essere sentitu." When I speak I want to be listened to.

This sense of male dignity is fostered by the family structure. The unquestionable authority in the family is the father. His views are not subject to challenge. His word has a brutal effect. His rage thunders down on the children and their mother. The children retaliate by tyrannizing their juniors; they play games in which the toys of the loser are destroyed by the winner. As wives, mothers, sisters, daughters,and fiancées, women are claimed by different men. But fundamentally, they are owned by a father, and it is prudent for a stranger to keep that fact in mind.

As a good wife, a Noro woman is submissive, passive, cloistered. Her vision of Italy is the street on which she lives. The warning of her priest during childhood and her isolation at the first signs of puberty contribute to her passivity in adulthood. Although she meets community standards of virtue, her restraint creates unsatisfactory relationships with her husband.

-15-

Maria is a typical Noro housewife, a good woman. From her woman's perspective, she understands the same network of power that the men have described. Of her daily life, she says:

As soon as I get up I clean the house. Then I prepare something for my husband and by that time the children come for theirs. When I wash, the whole day slips by, I am on my feet all the time. The men come home like wolves. Particularly with the tomato crop. You cannot even see them. So every day they want to be changed. The evening passes quickly. Then at eleven, maybe midnight, I go to bed. Sometimes I have my feet on the ground at four in the morning.

When one knows how to struggle there is no scarcity. Look how my children grumble in the morning that they are sleepy. I say to them: do you want money on Sunday ? There is this nuisance of the movies. So they get up. Without money the priest does not sing Mass.

After the girl died on me and six months had passed, this man came around to all his friends asking for votes. Paoli, he said to my husband, you have to do me this favor. We played as children together. You have to give me your vote. My husband said to him: Yes, but what I have in my stomach I must tell you. Do you remember that day when I had come to get to you and you turned around like a dog? He answered: Sometimes one does not know how things in life really are. My head was confused and I acted that way. But for any need you have you can count on me because I have friends.

You see there are votes from the entire family: my mother, my brothers, Zi Raffaele, and many cousins. We have a whole heap of relatives. A vote must be given to someone, but not to one who does nothing for us.

Some time afterward the hospital bill for my girl arrived and my husband gave it to him. And he said: Rest assured you will not have to pay a cent. Up to this time, nothing else has come. May be years will pass and then some paper will arrive. A bill arrived for my grandmother after she had been dead for ten years.

I praise Zia Jachinedda. She minds her own business. It is better when there are things to do and not start latching yourself to the thoughts of others.

The emotional ingredients of this Sicilian poverty are: a never ending improvisation and conniving in order to make ends meet; a feeling of isolation from the mainstream of life; a point where a man becomes a thing that neither laughs nor grieves.

The children appear gripped by a permanent frenzy. They scheme and they steal. They acquire habits that doom them to becoming school dropouts. Nine-year-old Bepino is a typical case. His father is a day laborer who unleashes his rage during the rare moments of communication with his son. Bepino has six brothers and sisters. The nine of them live in one room, but with string and cloth several cubicles have been fashioned to divide the sexes among the children and them from the parents. Bepino scrounges around for food during the day. When he returns at night, he gets two slices of bread and a whack in the mouth if he takes more.

His mother is always in black. So many relatives have died in quick succession that she tinted her dress black once and for all. That was so long ago the original color begins to show. His oldest sister is also in mourning, which added to the arrival of menstruation means she is isolated from the other children and the community.

Bepino's teachers live outside the community, even though this is against the law. But their position gives them influence. They arrive by train or automobile at eight in the morning and flee at one in the afternoon. Their method of instruction consists of having the children copy numbers and letters. In the third grade, they begin to memorize concepts. When the teacher asks what snow is, the children answer as though they were saying their catechism. They learn ancient history in this way; they have never seen the Greek temple a few kilometers away.

Bepino was totally unprepared for school when he enrolled at the age of six. He had never made a drawing, had never listened to a story, and had never seen a picture book, had never held a pencil in his hand. He is repeating second year for the third time. He is intelligent but restless and mischievous. He still cannot read. Bepino learned quickly that if he arrived late at school, his teacher would wave him out of the room. He is unlikely to repeat second grade for a fourth time; his father will take him into the fields.

The mountain that shelters Noro on the North resembles the head of a cocker spaniel with its jaw resting on the plain. Halfway down, the houses of the village look like a pile of debris. The single road disappears into the low silhouette of the town core and then emerges into the plain on the way to the sea. Most of the labor force works in different stages of agricultural production and distribution. The next sizable group is in construction. The remainder includes artisans, shopkeepers, and street peddlers. Many of the wives sew in their homes and sell their work to a middleman. Some of the children are hired out as apprentices. Statistics hide the considerable part-time trading that goes on;

the trading involves an outlay of many hours of work for a pittance.

Daily routine for the unemployed depends on whether they are old or young. The young men may manage to get out of bed by eleven and make exploratory contacts at the town center. At one o'clock it is back home for lunch. At five in the afternoon, the shutters open and out they come again, more bored than ever, and kill time recounting amorous adventures or playing cards. At dusk, back home again for supper and then into the street once more until midnight, when the day may be capped with a collective _pisciata_ against the wall to see who goes highest. The winner is the most virile.

The older men are more prompt in reaching their stations around the grubby _piazza_: in the shade during summer and in the sun during winter. Their talk is mostly about the past. And the past is often several incidents discussed over and over with different embellishments. The present they note in their critical faces. From a distance, they appear to be patiently waiting for death.

The neat social distinctions that exist in Noro belie a first impression of poverty's equality. The most respectable are those who seem to do nothing but apparently live well. God knows where their money comes from. And it is nobody's business. Next come the _professionisti_--physicians, lawyers, druggists. Then come those in agriculture: landowners, sharecroppers, tenants, laborers. At rock bottom are those who take care of someone else's cattle. The elite poor are those on the poor list, the _elenco dei poveri_, which entitles them to certain free services. The list is compiled annually by the town administration after much jockeying in the community. Its compilers do not ignore vote-getting possibilities in assigning names on the list. About a third of the inhabitants are on it.

Noro's government pivots around a semi-permanent coalition of Christian Democrats and Communists. Changing combinations of smaller political parties support the core group. These shifting alliances may appear chaotic, but one has to keep in mind the difference between noisy rhetoric and decision-making in locked rooms. The political fragmentation, besides, provides the pleasure of conflict.

The canon in the western world of an ever better economic and moral future in unknown in the world of Noro. The Noro reality is the mafia mentality of trading favors.

****

Many of the poor in these Southern towns abandon them and move to the slums of Northern cities. In the lexicon of western economists,

-18-

this act marks the first step toward progress. The people in this vast migration are the silent but willing partners of the policymaker. Their voices are muted. In the learned discussion of economics, they comprise a statistic. Their entrance into modern life is via the railroad station. Into the street they go with the family heirloom luggage, bringing a new language and creating a new tension. They are the blacks of American society entering the machine of modern industrialization.

Trilano, where I searched for migrants from Noro, is the step to the better life. My sixth floor room in the city faced a courtyard. Noises bounced off the walls and fused as they climbed upward; they were not rude sounds and did not last long into the night as they do in a big city of the South. Children laughing, a masseur smacking a body; a typewriter; the gurgle of flushing toilets; music played on a phonograph. The noises would subside and then rise unexpectedly, one afternoon to the accompaniment of a record of Ponchielli's Dance of the Hours.

Many of the migrants live in squalid shanties without plumbing or garbage collection. The innovations in Trilano include kidnapping and political terrorism. The Southerners make a noteworthy contribution to these activities.

Speaking of the different life he has found here, Giuseppe says:

> Down there in Noro, there are certain restrictions on women. There are questions of honor. If a woman cuckolds a man she may be killed. Up here she is generally thrown out of the house and that is that. If violence is done by one of these people up here, it is all right. But if one of us from the South does it, so much the worse. So we tread carefully.

> We hang around here and there. Sometimes we go to dance halls. When it is over the women go their way and we go ours. To get women we walk the streets. Some want too much. If they ask for ten thousand, we go for a long walk.

Paolina is the grand protectress of these prostitutes. Of her profession and enlightened modern law, she says:

> They commit no crime. The criminality comes from the men who interpret the law. If a prostitute commits a crime why isn't her customer brought before the Tribunal? The law closed the bordellos and told the women: you are now free. The identity lists were abolished and with it

the ability to control venereal disease. They were forced
into the streets where they have to protect themselves
from male violence. And their identification still continues, legal or not. Stefania got a job as a cleaning
woman. In ten days she was fired because her boss found
out she was a whore.

Stefania describes her introduction into the occupation:

> My mother threw me out of the house because I went
> to the amusement park alone. So I took off. A man was
> watching me at the bus stop. Oh, you are not waiting
> for any bus he said. I have been watching you for an
> hour. Tell me the truth. I will treat you like a bro-
> ther. I was afraid. He told me there was nothing to
> fear. He took me to a room behind a store. There was
> a clean bed. He caressed me and I reached for him.
> The next day he brought me to the railroad station.
> There were some girls there and one of them came up to
> me and told me the place was theirs. I told them that
> there were more than enough benches. They talked among
> themselves and then one of them came over and said: all
> right, go do your thing. And that's how I got started.

Trilano is a center of high fashion. At the other end of the female
spectrum, Lisa, a model, can by her entrance into a busy dining room reduce the high decibels to zero. She describes her life as a series of
contemptuous reactions against males.

> I have known different men--English, German, French--
> but the greatest exploiter is the Italian male. He is in
> search of a lover not a wife. That is his fantasy. He
> captures an Italian girl; but it is no great conquest.
> She puts together a strategy of femininity. Soon after
> the marriage, the lover fantasy disappears. He needs some-
> one to iron his shirts, go do the marketing, the cooking.
> So he goes out to find another lover. And the girl's
> strategy of combing her hair, dressing up, walking with
> bouncing buttocks, reinforcing the male fantasy, backfires
> on her.

> I do not want to be sucked into this Italian love.
> When I get amorous feelings I replace them with contempt;
> for then I can control the situation. Let them pay homage
> by bringing me jewelry.

And so power still underlies the human relationship, albeit under shifting moral and legal codes. The Italian obsession with power takes on a new dimension. Moreover, it becomes more complex and more based on arms-length dealings. And, as we will see in the forthcoming chapters, this evolution of power sets the scene of a modern mafia world of manipulation through massive systems of control.

Angelo--I met him at a construction site--exemplifies an array of characteristics one identifies with Italian rural character: scrupulous honesty, a high motivation for working, suspicion of society, distrust of authority. But there are anomalies and paradoxes. The government should set up a commission to fix wages. Man is good, but corrupting and corruptible. If a man takes an interest in your affairs, he can only be up to no good. Angelo is anticlerical and religious, antigovernment and ready to give government more powers. He does not know the economic jargon, but in flashes of insight he describes the underlying nature of economic events.

He says:

We are strangers in this city. The people speak a different dialect. Where I came from people greet each other morning, noon, and night. You meet a person and say: let us kiss hands. Here you greet a person and he does not answer.

You trust nobody in this city. I met someone on the tram I never saw before. Where are you going, he said. To Noro. So am I. We got to the railroad station. He offered to buy the tickets. He said he had no small bills and I gave him some notes. He started to walk in the direction away from the ticket office. I grabbed him by the shirt. Had I let him go another ten feet he would have screwed me out of my money.

Noro is beautiful, but here there is more work. I earn more. True, one consumes more too. But I always have some money in my pocket. The bosses are not always on your back. When you first come here it seems like nobody is working. But they accomplish more even though nobody seems to be doing anything.

The workers who come to Trilano from the region of Noro make the shift by a system of chain migration. Those already established in the city pave the way for new migrants by finding lodging for them and providing them with job information. In this way, the abrupt change is more manageable. They come with no family, no industrial skills, and little idea of what occupation to pursue. In Noro, they worked at their own pace. In Trilano, their work is subdivided and its rhythm is set by superiors.

Ciccina sums up the simultaneous haven and trap that Trilano represents for the migrants. She says:

I was born in Noro. I really do not know how many people live in that place. I was never in a city until I came here. My father was a barrel maker. I was never in a schoolroom. Not even for one day. My father had six children. Only the eldest went to school.

When I was twenty-four years old, I married a man of the village. He abandoned me after fifteen months. Without saying a word. And so I do not ask about him and he does not inquire about me. Why should I? What has he done for me? He did not give me a piece of ribbon.

One day I told him: Look, when I have to live and work just to give you something to live, I prefer working and living alone. He beat me.

I have three children. One is a pleasure to the eyes. She looks like a doll. And I have one who is not even five months old. The eldest is at the head of her class. I say to the Lord give her health to study.

My husband is here in Trilano. He has a woman at Piazza Napoli, at the last stop of the "L" bus. We have used the law against him, but he tells the judge that he does not work. There was a trial and he was convicted. He appealed his conviction. His people appeared for him in court. And they put a noose around his neck. For their slips of the tongue he got twenty days in jail. When the judge saw that he was condemning himself, he told him: Enough Cannoni. He said to the judge: Listen, I Cannoni Nicola, would send her five and sometimes ten, and would send them in the mail. No, I answered. Not even once by mail. He would send them with the laborers working with him.

When I had enough, I left the children in a boarding school and went away. I came alone. I went to the Sisters and said: Look, my husband has gone and abandoned me. How can I manage? I have just left the hospital for an operation behind the ear. I live on the commune as an indigent. But I can go to the North. I can do some work because here one dies of hunger. Then the Mother Superior, since she knows me, since my people are all professors--I alone am no good--said: Ciccina, bring the children.

I went down to the City Hall to take out the necessary

-22-

documents. Then I took the children to the nuns. Fifteen
days later I came up here. I left the children at the
collegio on the sixth day of May and left on the twenty-
ninth. The small one and the big one did not want to stay.
So I told them: So you want to go home? You will die of
hunger because I have no work. The oldest one insisted.
I will break your head, I told her. She picked up courage
and decided to stay. What should I have said to her?

She wrote me a letter. On the 29th of June, on the
feast of Saints Peter and Paul, she had her first communion.
Dear Mama, she wrote. I thought you would be here. Instead,
grandmother acted as mother for me. I would have liked to
see you, if only for a few hours. How could I possibly have
gone down. It takes too much money.

To find a job, I went to the Chamber of Labor at Corso
Buenos Aires. I began to work on the 12th of June. But I do
not want to be a domestic anymore. They abuse me. I used to
weigh sixty kilos. Look at me now. Going up and down all
those stairs. At the hotel, I start at eight in the morning,
stop at noon and begin again at six. Often they call me
back at three. I want to find a job in a factory.

Life here is different from down there. We could not
speak with a man there. They would quickly say: Look at that
bitch. You understand, because of jealousy. And watch out
if you dared wear some lipstick! Living here is better. Who
knows the difference if you are a domestic. I sleep in a
private house. We are three women in a room.

If someone here asks me do you want to go to a movie,
I can go. Down there, everybody knows everybody else's
business. In Noro, if by chance my husband spoke to a
woman, it would quickly get around by the time he arrived
home. Especially since they know I am jealous. So when
he got back I would be silent. He would notice and say:
What has happened? Nothing I would answer. And then he
would beat me.

My mother told me he is here with a woman. I got his
phone number and dialed. Pronto, he answered. Who is
this, I answered. And he answers who is this also. He
knew who it was. He knows me well. Even when I do not
speak in Sicilian. He hung up.

Then this morning I took the bus and went up there.
He saw me and did not come out. He was white with fear.

Because I could have him arrested, I can say he abandoned
me with three children. A policeman I know told me that.

Look at my nose. He did it with his mouth. In a blind
rage. He told me one night that he wanted to go away. He
could not free his hands because I was holding him. So he
bit me.

It is late. Can I go?

The quality and cost of the living quarters of these migrants vary.
There is on the record an apartment of six rooms rented to forty migrants.
In one construction barracks, the cots were without sheets and placed end
to end about two feet apart. The stench made conversation indoors difficult. In spite of such conditions, stories like those of Angelo and
Ciccina explain why the migrants continue to pour in from the South. And
because they do, they are fair game for urban exploiters. Rents vary
from as little as a sixth of a migrant's wages for a controlled apartment to as much as a third. Landlords infrequently are from the upper
classes; they are mostly skilled workers born in Trilano, who do not per-
mit their Marxism to interfere with making a fast lira.

The portion of wages not needed for subsistence goes back to Noro.
Newer migrants save as much as half their pay. They react more readily
to the suggestion that they are neglecting their families. A letter of
lament from home brings a quick response. Occasionally, an unscrupulous
member of the clan exploits this sensitivity. Sometimes family members
travel the long distance to Trilano to check and report back.

The job broker, the _mediatore_, has arisen out of the influx of
these people into Trilano. He is generally a former worker from the
South who can barely sign his name but dresses in flashy clothes and
drives the latest model automobile. Migrants are introduced to him by
a _paesano_ from the same village. They get a once-over, and, if found
acceptable, are referred to an employer. It is often made clear that
hiring is contingent upon giving up fringe benefits. Such a contract is
illegal but common.

A migrant's social contacts are confined to his fellow townsmen,
the _paesani_. He manages to find at work or his rooming house the people
who come from his town. Without such contacts, he feels isolated.
There are difficult barriers in dealing with the Trilanesi. The grammar
and ideas in their respective languages are not the same. On the train,
a migrant cuts some bread and offers it to his fellow passengers. A Tri-
lanese asks him if he always carries a knife. The migrant speaks poor
Italian and is sensitive to exposing himself to a situation in which he

would lose face. He moves between the railroad station that brought him into the new world, his room, and his job. Much of the departure from this routine movement involves meanderings in search of women.

The new migrants consider their transfer temporary. I will go back, they say, when a job is available down there. The environment there is more human. But in actuality the longer they stay, the less likely is their return, particularly if they marry in the North. With the coming of children, they break out of their closed circle. The old town in the South becomes an occasional qualm of conscience assuaged by increasingly irregular gifts of money sent home to ease a sense of guilt.

Their jobs are at the lower levels of the labor force: unskilled labor in construction, factory hands, service employment including some peddling. In time, they enter occupational training programs and rise up the occupational ladder in industry. Some of those in construction become craftsmen. The higher the occupational level and the younger the migrant, the more he expresses satisfaction with his job.

Many of these migrants who bring their families settle in the improvised quarters at the city's edge. One is an abandoned dairy converted into a multiple-family dwelling. The children play in the fetid water that settles in the court yard. Hastily put together partitions trap the combined odor of mold, clothing saturated with perspiration, garbage, urine, and feces.

To sum up, life in Noro is relatively simple and more genuine, even while it depends on unspoken arrangements of power. The new life in Trilano, astronomically more complex, dresses the same arrangements in modern clothes. Life in both places is based on the same mafia principle of power broking. But the one in Trilano is more insidious because it is less accessible.

So much in the way of prologue. We next go across the sea where the mafia principle emerges in still more modern guise.

Chapter 2

The Mafia is Everywhere

Is there a mafia in the United States? Sure there is. The mafia
is everywhere in society. Every organization is a mafia racket. _Mafiosi_
of non-Italian origin latch on to parent-teacher associations, transportation authorities, military establishments, academic disciplines, trade
unions, industrial corporations, the office of the United States presi-
dency---you name it---and operate them as conspiratorial organizations
serving the power needs of those who control them. Their success derives
from creating and defending an exclusive operation. Mafia syndicates dislike competition and publicity. They prefer the quiet life. Most university presidents, for instance, have the reputation of never having
uttered a provocative idea. They manage ongoing rackets for government
and industry under the guise of research and education. The clean-cut
Machiavellians who recommend techniques of manipulation to public
officials are obviously mafia types. So are the managers of industrial
corporations.

The key to success in society is creating and defending an exclusive
racket. It is a universal practice, employed even by intellectuals who
reassemble old ideas, give them new language, develop good connections in
the media, and protect the reconstituted thoughts from poachers. The
ideas may be nonsense, yet they survive, provided that they acquire a
reputation for profundity. Some intellectuals, having obtained notoriety
for supposedly unique ideas, dare not arrange them intelligibly. Clarity
would be their undoing, exposing them as platitudes.

Each syndicate has its own kind of violence. What is proper for a
local union president certainly would not befit a college president.
Moreover, all syndicates suffer the turbulence triggered by the passing
of the boss. But once the in-fighting subsides with the choice of a
successor from carefully culled aspirants to leadership, the violence
simmers down to the accustomed level for that particular syndicate.
Each leader, or _capo_, delineates his area of interest, respects the duchies
of others, and avoids dislocating the operations of another _capo_. Poaching

-26-

only begets disequilibrium. To maintain decorum, each chief uses a lieutenant. Whether referred to as vice-president for academic affairs, executive director, staff assistant, presidential aide, or consigliere, he holds primary responsibility for vigilance against the foragers who collect at the fringes of the chief's jurisdiction. On the basis of who can be screwed most easily, the consigliere distributes through the organization the stresses caused by the chief's obsessions. In keeping with the dignity of presidential office, the dirty tricks covertly sanctioned by the capo are performed at the lieutenant's own peril.

This live-and-let-live philosophy breaks down when a capo gets bad publicity. Wounded by such rotten luck, he often seeks to protect himself at the expense of other mafiosi, generating thereby a scramble for cover. The solid ranks disintegrate as all begin to testify against each other. The first who confesses acquires high honors. Only traditional mafiosi practice omertà. They are honorable men and can be trusted.

From time to time, cooperating syndicates congregate, ascribe a sublime mission to their operations, and bestow honors upon each other. Honors take the form of inscribed names on buildings, plaques, gold medals, scrolls, gold keys, board chairmanships, and honorary degrees. When prominent mafiosi in legitimate society congregate to celebrate a public event, they are called dignitaries. Less respectable syndicates hold their conventions in secluded areas. There the assembled chiefs of cooperating syndicates understand and honor each other. But the principle is the same.

This is the mafia mentality that pervades the economy. It exists in the auto industry, in pharmaceuticals, in construction, in banking, in the oil industry and the dairy business. In public education, for example, the interests of bureaucracies and organized teachers predominate. The major task is making quiet deals. In addition, the rackets in the economy often divide along ethnic lines. Thus Jews nest in motion pictures, while corporate executives who offer bribes as a business practice are generally Wasps. And despite the relatively small percentage of Irish Catholics in the United States, an Irish mafia runs the Catholic church.

The government bureaucracy has one of the most lucrative rackets in the economy. Double dippers flourish. Those who feed at the public trough work without allegiance to productivity and increase their compensation by command through the taxing power. Contrary to popular belief, they get substantially higher pay than private sector employees in comparable jobs. They vote for themselves lush pension rights. Through projects such as training programs, they supplement their incomes. In one such program at a hideaway ski lodge, after a dinner of aged prime ribs of beef slowly roasted on a bed of rock salt, I was scheduled to speak on the subject of government economy.

There are mafia cliques in university structures, too. At a well-known university in the East, there is one nesting in the College of Business. The formal organization chart reveals neither who its members are nor who make the crucial decisions. The family comprises a chief, two consiglieri, and four hit men from the instructor staff assigned to dirty tricks. They call the shots on promotions and awards. Advisory services come from the behavioral sciences.

These examples illustrate that the essence of American enterprise is organization, and the end of organization is exclusion and control to assure a steady flow of returns. This is Sicilian mafia philosophy pure and simple. Moreover, the exclusion and control exercised by the economy's legitimate syndicates divert managerial talent into illegitimate activity. Consequently, the bold innovators in contemporary life are to be found in the ranks of the more bloody illegitimate mafia.

In the legitimate mafia, this function of exclusion and control is called planning. In the illegitimate mafia, the same technique is referred to as keeping things in the family. In the legitimate mafia, government and corporation spawn a nepotism that produces disabling mutations. The illegitimate mafia nurtures the ebbing entrepreneurship in society and provides a tonic for tired Wasp blood. As a corollary, the Sicilians who made the successful transplant from their island had fertile new soil in which to work. As a second corollary, the difference between respectable and unrespectable society can be reduced by legitimizing the services of unrespectable society.

The routine procedures characteristic of the mafia are common throughout the legitimate society. Agreements over prices and spheres of influence are tacit; as the old mafia soon learned, spelling out an accord in writing only invites complications. Accommodation with political authorities is achieved through such time-tested procedures as going to parties, sharing plane rides, and meeting in faraway places. Even the solution of last resort---wiping out the competition---is an operating tool in the highest economic and political circles of society.

The differences in product between the two subsocieties---autos versus prostitution, for example---are mere accidents of history. They should not obscure the fact that the system is mafia oriented. The degree to which illegitimate mafiosi find sympathetic spirits in the system is a measure of their affinity for each other. The awarding of honorary degrees to crooked politicians supports this view. So does the resolution of a former Attorney General to stop using pejorative terms in referring to Italian-American criminals.

While the illegitimate mafia makes little pretense about the nature of the service it renders, members of the Wasp mafia in legitimate society pose as public servants while busy getting theirs. A greater sense of noble purpose prevails in their ranks. Should this pose be insufficient to soften their perturbations of Protestant conscience, Wasps support activities of churches and boys' clubs. A critical difference between a Wasp crook and an ethnic crook lies in the fact that the one, having worked at it longer over the generations has more finesse and more competence in getting the law to promote his interests. But the two also differ in their ability to keep cool. For example, a sociologist notes that Wasps rank lowest among different cultural groups in controlling themselves at the dark street corners of black neighborhoods. But no hard data exist on this matter.

Judgments about what is good and what is evil, however, often arise from entrenched but unexamined habits of thinking. The evil associated with the unsystem of the illegitimate mafia can be eliminated by revised thinking. What is considered evil can be revised to appear good. About the traditional mafia, for example, one can reorient one's thinking by looking upon the word as an acronym for Make A Friend with an Italian Association. One can also borrow a lesson from blacks and Jews by organizing a NAAIP (National Association for the Advancement of Italian People) or IAL (Italian Anti-Defamation League). Try giving me a compelling reason why Italians as well as Blacks and Jews should not organize and grab a few positions in the system. Equity demands that every group in the economy be given its quota of top posts. Wasps and Jews have exceeded their share and should be cut back. As a gesture of consistency and in a spirit of liberalism, the university professors who advocate percentage quotas should support a quota system for their own profession. Those evicted from the legitimate mafia by such fair dealing could be resettled under government programs into the illegitiamte mafia. Is there a better way to promote integration? Italian-Americans would claim ten percent of all professorial posts and university presidencies. Thus the obsolete liberal ethic can be refurbished by assimilating disadvantaged intellectuals into the university mafia.

In one area, the illegitimate mafia outshines the legitimate. Illegitimate mafiosi provide services more freely chosen by their customers. Those hawked by producers in the system are supported by the manipulation of advertising. Accordingly, the subeconomy behaves in a way more consistent with traditional economic theory. However, illegitimate producers do not have the services of economics professors. The professors are too busy teaching obsolete economics to provide the illegitimate producers a supporting faith. Long-run equilibrium is attained as the two economies move toward each other. At that point, both economies become unresponsive to the welfare of consumers. But in the short run, consumer sovereignty rules the illegitimate economy.

In short, the real difference between the mafia in the system and the mafia in the unsystem is only a lag in respectability. What other differences, for instance, are there between an auto executive who makes souped-up cars for young males of modest intellect and a mafia entrepreneur running a numbers racket?

Violence in the unsystem is an act of feeling. Violence in the system is more calculated. Thus, the cigarette industry condemns the use of statistical technique in drawing an association between lung cancer and cigarette smoking and approves the same method in discerning relationships between sales and advertising. Violence in the unsystem is messy. In the system, violence is discreet because of the remoteness of the victim.

Although members of the unsystem progress, in their amicable relations with local public officials, toward legitimizing their violence, they have devoted insufficient time to cultivating cordial associations with national officials. Illegitimate mafiosi at best can count on the cordiality of a mayor or governor when they get into trouble. Their public relations are wanting. With improved public relations, they can blur the distinction between system and unsystem.

In accord with academic practice in the field of economics, I shall henceforth call the legitimate mafia economy "LME and its illegitimate offspring "IME." The major elements of LME are the corporation, the government, and the university. These elements become increasingly linked with each other, and, by a process of leveling down, government and university adopt the methods and morality of the corporation. In IME, the names of incumbents suggest how Italian-American criminals sensitive to equal opportunity law have recruited and uplifted low class blacks and Latin Americans. LME favors middle class technology such as lying, bribery, light burglary, wire tapping, fraudulent use of the mails, bugging, character assassination, and obstruction of justice. In IME, less sophisticated technology prevails.

In both of these economies, the production and consumption of goods generate positive and negative results. A noteworthy contrast between them lies in these positive-negative relationships. In LME, the bad tends to rise relative to its good; in IME good rises relative to bad. Thus, the auto business produces positive results in flexible means of transportation, and negative results in pollution, noise, ugliness, and mechanized human relationships. The numbers racket in IME generates good in promoting a sense of expectations among the poor and bad in provoking an occasional fracas.

A noteworthy factor causing LME negative results to rise disproportionately is the inexorable pressure in the legitimate system to maintain consumer demand. The need to prop up demand thus created gas guzzlers and polluting soap detergents that clean whiter than white. LME is pressured by the imperative to convince the public that an intake of chemicals is the sure road to love and happiness. It would seem, then, that an LME firm is able to maintain profits in relation to its ability to maximize negative side effects. To assure profits, the firm has to increase social costs. An upper limit is reached as these costs kill off a rising number of consumers and thereby invite government intervention.

In LME, the bad accordingly is sustained by society until its members muster sufficient strength to curtail them. In IME, where the good is outlawed, the negative aspects even though proportionately less important, are cited as proof of the need to prohibit its wares. In IME, moreover, negatives are almost exclusively imposed on racketeers in the form of beatings and homicides but hardly ever on the consumer. The high demand for its outlawed goods increases the resources required to curtail the demand. The control of the bad, as for example prostitution, is achieved more efficiently by legalizing the good. Assuming rationality on the part of the system, the legalization occurs when the cost of prohibiting the illegitimate goods exceeds the costs of allowing them to enter LME.

LME is more efficient than IME in the exploitation of persons. Its guiding morality is feasibility. In IME, traditional rural notions prevail, such as that persons are worthy of respect and lose their worth when they fail to behave in accordance with moral principle. There is on the whole greater authenticity in IME. The relationships in LME are more fraudulent.

Legitimate mafiosi and their lieutenants who get caught with their pants down have greater redress. They can employ connections in government and corporate circles, invoke executive and constitutional privilege, obtain a presidential pardon. If necessary, they can hire clever lawyers. During the long judicial process, they can write best sellers, get themselves interviewed on television for a fee, or give lectures at universities where sociology students are ready with bags of money for instant insight. The most lucrative deal is the best seller. An LME paperback in its twelfth printing is a tribute to the sharply honed technique of profit maximization, a bellwether of the willingness of a writer to employ such technology, and an index of the rising number of semiliterates graduated by LME's schools of learning.

Half of the goods produced by LME are either worthless, harmful, or sold under fraudulent pretense. As the consumption of such goods rises, so do the indicators of human misery. The society goes downhill as the indicator of progress, the gross national product, rises. While the sale of shoddy and misrepresented goods provides momentum to LME, IME serves consumer preferences with greater authenticity. Differences in output, it must be emphasized, are an accident of history. The Anglo-Americans and German-Americans settled in the wilderness first. The Brahmins in LME need not use the tougher tactics of their ancestors to maintain their position. Secluded in corporate board rooms, they employ more genteel measures. The earthy tactics of their forefathers are no longer needed.

A more virulent entrepreneurship prevails in IME. Their leaders can provide lessons in effective business administration; the Harvard University Graduate School of Business would profit from hiring IME crooks as guest lecturers. But LME prefers a process of percolation rather than confrontation. In this way, the timid managers in LME impose the costs of their quietly drawn policies on those with the least influence. Pollution provides the example. By any index, the poor lived in pollution long before bored female suburbanites and their child revolutionaries discovered the stuff. Well-fed young radicals sing anti-pollution songs to the ear splitting accompaniment of instruments amplified by power from polluting plants. The poor get caught in two ways: by the deflection of resources away from them and by the rise in costs of their goods and services. But for the demonstrators, ecology is an antidote to boredom. Who knows if a point of view on poverty may appear, reflected in such slogans as: Don't flatten that cockroach, brother; we need to maintain the ecological balance.

Despite evidence to the contrary, there is a presumption of harmony between the interests of LME producers and those of the public. The history of economics in the past one hundred years is an account of a grudging retreat from this belief. The predatory effects of LME were dismissed as externalities, meriting at best a footnote. LME enjoyed a sympathetic press. Economics textbooks gave its depredations moral sanction. British-American economic theory is an extraordinary intellectual feat of rationalizing greed and envy. In sophomore economics, the neat supply and demand curves on the blackboard sanctify the system. Their logic is impeccable but their assumptions are contrary to the facts.

Jointly and unilaterally, corporation and state manage the public in the interest of maintaining the institutions of LME. Should the corporation fail through its propaganda to generate sufficient demand for its goods, the state fills the breach. Their management, moreover, is exercised at increasing psychological cost to the individual.

It takes more than modest skills to raise the consumer each year to fever pitch. In the automobile industry, bumpers, hoods, fenders, grilles, and glass in new shapes trigger the annual drooling. Advertising in LME is a measure of what it takes to prepare the consumer to exercise his sovereignty. If the corporation fails in such preparation, the government throws its forces of monetary and fiscal policies into the fray. The corporate tactic includes three stages: in the first, LME's mass media condition the public to believe that the sure road to Nirvana is the consumption of goods. In the second stage, LME managers determine which particular product could foster this conviction. In the third, the forces of irrationality are mustered through advertising to lock in this relationship and manage it thereafter. In the trial of combat between producer and consumer, the producer has the greater resources. Not least in importance among them is greater information.

The resources of LME mafiosi include money, connections, property and skills. Money and connections are critical resources in determining position in the hierarchy. Money is the most crucial of these assets.

Money can buy the others. Moreover, the amount of funds a manager controls reflects the wisdom of his opinion. The reasoning of a manager controlling twice as much money as another renders his opinion twice as weighty. An expression of idiocy by a prominent prince of power is treated in the same fashion as the emperor's new clothes. Those who wield big money and who are on record as accepting the system get cabinet positions in the national government.

Money is therefore the supreme weapon. One can buy almost everyone and everything if the price is right. With money friendships are bought, politicians corrupted, intellectuals purchased. Advertising money can induce fears in the sovereign consumer and suggest a panacea to allay them. Money shapes public tastes, determines what is reality, fixes the frontiers of knowledge. Money buys honors, privileges, justice, strong men, beautiful women, honorary degrees. Money is cold. Little sentimentality is wasted on those who lack it. Money converts politics from an act of moral consensus to one of cruelty. With money, one can control communication lines, acquire recognition for accomplishments, and achieve immortality. If men lose their sense of cause, money in LME can buy mercenaries to support movements. Money determines the quality of justice. There is good justice for those with lots of money and modest justice for those with limited amounts of money. Not all individuals augment their judicial clout with tidy sums of money. But the ability to control judicial decisions that affect one's interest is inconceivable without resources.

Monetary considerations thus vitally affect relationships in LME. The amount of money in transactions measures the importance of these relationships. The producer amasses more money to achieve his objectives than the consumer does to defend his interests. The consumer can more effectively get his due through actions as a seller. A producer has greater resources with which to expand sales than the consumer commands to protect his welfare from actions of the producer. The institutions of LME are geared to the maintenance of its production machinery. The imperative of increased sales requires the perpetration of fraud. For the consumer, the more effective weapon against such deception is the utilization of similar practices as a seller. We are told that the consumer makes choices after a rational weighing of options. In fact, his choices are conditioned by LME managers who seek to instruct the consumer about what his needs are. Intelligence and education can serve to undermine LME by creating resistance to such manipulation.

The billions of dollars poured annually into advertising foster the chicanery necessary to maintain LME. Producers must convince the consumer that their products are needed, that no better ones exist, and that the consumer would suffer deprivation if he did not buy them. Whether or not the offer is genuine is irrelevant. The valid consideration is not whether a product promotes consumer welfare, but whether the buyer thinks it does. This persuasion may not be achieved. Government represents the ideal world of the seller. It provides services whether the buyer wants them or not, and it punishes him if he does not pay for them. For certain classes of products--such as weapons systems--the government makes decisions meeting the needs of the armed services and supplying firms and then employs propaganda to persuade the public of the wisdom of its commitments. One can draw from such experience an axiom of the mafia principle that the use of chicanery is commendable to the degree that its use achieves a desired result. Honesty is irrelevant in LME. Impact is what counts.

The corporate art of deception penetrates the larger society. The populace reduces the falsification of reality by molding its behavior to reflect the falsified version of reality. In a Pirandellian maneuver, the unreal thus becomes real. The government asserts that the right to lie is necessary for survival. The university joins forces in the creation of imagery by offering its skills in doing so to LME. The undergirding of the system rests on deception.

The contributions made to such artful contrivance by each LME mafioso foster the common interest of the system. In the automobile industry, whether the consumer heeds the call by selecting General Motors, Ford, or Chrysler is irrelevant to the national interest so long as he succumbs to the blandishment. Moreover, the success of the industry as a whole assures production in other sectors. Billions of dollars in highway construction correct the new traffic problems. The millions of accidents annually provide employment for auto repairmen, pharmacists, physicians, plastic surgeons, insurance carriers, attorneys, and undertakers. Thus, a decline in auto sales would seriously affect progress.

The gross national product is the Holy Grail of LME. The government cites the economic measure as a testimonial of progress. An overflowing garbage can is a tribute to the success of public officials in maintaining the GNP. To the tune of many billions of dollars, the GNP includes such items as cigarettes, booze, animal cosmetics, liquids and solids to nullify body odors, and psychiatric services to alleviate the consequences of progress as measured by the GNP. The fifty billion dollars in advertising, which also enters the national accounts, puts a price tag on the public's resistance to buy what is good for it. In transactions among themselves, the mafiosi of the different corporate and government sectors impose the costs of their settlements upon those who lack the syndical power to withstand such transfers.

The role of the mass media is of crucial importance in the promotion of these interests. As the fourth branch of government, the media have a need to sensationalize the problems and misfortunes of the princes of power. The need for sensationalism on the part of the media is

cloaked with the mantle of the public's right to know. Wary of such
publicity, managers prudently court the media's favor. Beneath the
surface hostility, however, the system's managers have a common
fascination for power, and like mafiosi in general, they understand
each other. With prudence, they can serve each other's interest in
amicable fashion.

The major concern of LME managers is the perennial one of the mafia:
how to maintain power within their respective duchies and how to guard
them from outside encroachment. The concern demands fealty to the
chief. Within each organization, a subordinate is judged on the basis
of whether his relations with superiors and outside managers favorably
affect the position of the chief. What is proper is that which maintains and enhances position in the hierarchy, and what is improper that
which undermines it. At the same time, the top managers must appear to
promote the needs of their respective constituencies.

Managerial decisions are an amalgam of views held by sub-monopolies
within the organization. Each sub-monopoly carries weight to the degree
that it can undermine the position of the chief. A frontal attack on a
threatening position is not prudent; it would be more effective for the
capo to isolate and weaken a standard bearer who challenges him.

Hypocrisy is a valuable asset for this task. Whether a person in
political office or in pursuit of one, whether an official in the public
or private sector or a university administrator, a clever manager does
not make the fatal error of describing matters as they are. Rather, he
depicts a reality suitable to maintain his power. Thus, when a professor
challenges a university president's policy, it would be more discreet to
curtail the challenger's initiative in the name of sub-monopolies in the
organization that sustain the president's views. The president can
quietly make such arrangements while keeping his own hands clean. He can
accordingly appear to be managing on the criterion of consent.

Some capi are too beholden to nobles in their organization. Such de-
pendence is undesirable even though it may rest on satisfying sentimental
grounds. These nobles may be carryovers from a previous administration
or new incumbents hired to assist the prince in establishing a power base.
Nevertheless, in order to reinforce his status in the hierarchy, the
prince must eliminate those by whose sufferance he lives and replace them
with obsequious subordinates. This purge can be carried out with impunity
so long as the prince persuades the nobles that he acts in their interest,
maintains in the course of eliminating them the support of the rank and
file, and avoids forcing the nobles to organize out of concern for their
future.

These tactics are common in both LME and IME. The official princes of power in LME--in government or out, corporate managers, university presidents--are essentially politicians. They must invent descriptions of reality that further their needs. From their promontory, the princes utter platitudes, often brilliantly. But genuine information is undercover.

For these reasons, one can lump together government and corporate organization. Obviously, there are differences. Corporations do not plunder through the power to tax. However, both government and private industry are political institutions that must control resources in a manner that sustains the organization. The issue raised in economics books of government planning versus corporate initiative is spurious. Both plan, and they do so in increasingly integrated fashion. They face similar internal rivalries. Although the imperative of profitability seems to be a difference, the distinction is not so sharp as it appears at first blush. In the long run, governments have to maintain some balance between revenue and expenditure, as do corporations. However, the forces of competition compel corporations to be more efficient in the use of resources. Only in a government office can an employee move from morning newspaper to extended coffee break and thence to early extended lunch.

On the surface, these oligarchs pose as benefactors; underneath the facade, they practice the art of extinguishing the careers of those not acceptable for entrance into a particular crime syndicate. The outstanding prince is one who outwardly appears to be a humanist while he discreetly acts to neutralize rivals below. He can perform this role wisely by assigning purges to an expendable subordinate. Again, we are dealing with procedures common to both IME and LME.

The managers of organization in LME maintain vigilance on each other, propose and dispose, and quietly, if at all possible, bargain out their differences. High government officials, former exponents of the people, serve as alter egos of organization managers. The people are spectators who pay for the performance of their agents. No significant changes in policy occur without the agreement or acquiescence of the affected chiefs. They shape public preferences, administer the armed state, and generally set the tone of American life. Their common source of irritation is an unmalleable constituency. Organized labor has not penetrated this circle in the same degree, but not because it does not aspire to. With greater responsiveness to the needs of the establishment, a deeper breakthrough is likely. Infiltrating the establishment, moreover, are university entrepreneurs, a tribe of professors that increases its prestige by the exercise of discretion and by convincing the managerial coteries that it possesses needed technical skill. Occasionally, low lifers from IME manage to penetrate the circle, should they have the physical and mental attributes acceptable to the club. The managers are so closely tied to the apparatus of state that it is difficult to determine on whose payroll they should be. They share a common problem of rendering ineffective the protestations that come from IME. Elected public officials exploit the protestations to acquire office and then tune their performance to the interests of the managerial hierarchies.

What are the origins of these capi in LME? They are predominantly of Anglo-Saxon Protestant stock. The pecking order is Wasp, facsimile Wasp, Northern European, and when the supply is scarce relative to demand, not-too-Jewish Jews and not-too-Negro blacks. Wasps predominate. They are in the Congress, the military, the top administrative posts of government, finance, and foreign policy. Affluent custodians of American values, they are suspicious of latter day Americans in IME. Spurred by noble feeling, they are disposed to use money to subvert the institutions they claim to support. The lineage they have built in the power positions of LME vies with that of Roman emperors.

Of the many syndicates in LME, one deserves special mention. And that is the official brains mafia drawn from banking, law, foundations, and Ivy League universities. United States presidents pick from its members as they choose from a display of vegetables. They give unto themselves the awesome responsibility of protecting American interests abroad. They have a reputation for sound judgment. But when one looks back over the decades, the decisions of the brains mafia have had disastrous consequences. They define the issues and manage the policies they formulate. While none of them have held a gun with a bullet bent on human destruction, they are real tough when it comes to committing the lives of others for causes they deem worthy. Their faces change over the years, but they come from the same club. Their common characteristic is the joy of power politics. Inaccessible to members of the unsystem, insensitive to popular concerns, the brains mafia nevertheless has the power to exercise a profound effect on the life of the citizen. The government rewards them with influential and prestigious posts; and when they leave their positions, no matter how disastrous their policies, they are rewarded with other prestigious positions in LME. The people cannot punish them for their mistakes.

Historically, Wasps have claimed the right to such power by virtue of their superior qualities. In the early years of the century, Senator Albert J. Beveridge from the State of Indiana was saying that God had been preparing the English and Teutonic people for a thousand years to govern inferior people. John W. Burgess, professor of political science at Columbia University, was asserting at the same time the right of the Anglo-Saxon race to assume leadership. Sociologist Edward A. Ross, disturbed by the immigrant waves of Catholics from Southern Europe, was saying:

> To the practiced eye, the physiognomy of certain
> groups unmistakably proclaims inferiority of type. I
> have seen gatherings of the foreign born in which narrow
> and sloping foreheads were the rule. The shortness and
> smallness of the crania were very noticeable.

Such arguments are disavowed today, but the attitudes arising from them
discreetly prevail.

The superior caste controls many devices with which to perpetuate
itself. For example, LME could not function without its retinue of
attorneys. The greater the monetary transactions involved, the greater
the need for expensive lawyers. The attorneys who protect the interests
of cheats, murderers, and thieves do not belong to the same class of
lawyers manning the ramparts of LME.

Unhappily, the mafia in LME is also taking over the rackets of
the traditional mafia. State and local governments are preempting the
horse betting business. A precedent has been established for cities
in financial distress to operate gambling casinos. As Las Vegas goes,
so do Atlantic City and Miami Beach. These events cause disorientation
among crooks in IME. What are they to do? LME does not like competition. So when the Las Vegas authorities refused entrance into their
city to a group of airline passengers with Italian names, it was no
accident. The straightforwardness of IME is not found in these legitimate operations. The gamblers supported by law in Nevada do not
quiver over providing free chips to working people who cash and bet
their paychecks. In Texas, mother of many legitimate mafiosi, the
Southwestern Bell Telephone Company has dossiers on the long-distance
calls of politicians. The utility dials into their telephone conversations without apprising the callers. In the firm's judgment, these
actions are within the legitimate performance of its business. Nevada
and Texas underscore the fuzzy distinction between LME and IME.

The mafia mentality has also invaded religious charities. While
information is difficult to obtain because of the separation of Church
and State, there is reason to think that Roman Catholic priests of
Irish ancestry operate lucrative rackets under the cloak of assisting
the poor. One of these organizations has acquired a reputation of
spending ninety percent of its receipts in administrative costs. Much
of the remainder goes toward the distribution of miraculous medals.

Thus, the few differences between the new and old mafia erode
with time. Equal opportunity law suggests how this drive toward same-
ness can be accelerated. The extraordinary managerial talent in IME

-38-

could be fused into LME by an amendment to the Civil Rights Act of 1964 to provide equal opportunity for traditional mafiosi to obtain positions in the hierarchal structure of LME. The managers so displaced in LME could be reassigned to the management of crime syndicates. Is there a better way to rejuvenate tired Wasp blood?

The development of a mass man in the service of LME begins at approximately age three in the life of an American child. At that time, the competing educational system in society--television--acquires a two-year advantage over the formal educational system in the preparation of the American mind. At an early stage in life, the child is prepared to enjoy mass culture and to pay for such amusement in docility to the demands of LME.

Thereafter, the child spends as much time before the television tube as he does in the traditional classroom. In the traditional classroom, a feeble and, in the main, useless, attempt is made to teach the child to think. In the alternate school of LME, the thinking is done for him. In the comfort of his living room, he is given instruction on the wonders of movies, sports, rock music, drugs, permissive sex, and sadism. He is taught an alternate language, the language of consumption, and an alternate ethic, the religion of instant gratification. While a few manage to escape, the alternate school develops in the typical child an aversion toward thinking and concentration.

Thus, television develops the biggest racket of them all by using a public trust of the airwaves to develop loyal soldiers. The medium does not simply provide programs, but an alternate culture that exerts a strong influence on literature and the interpreting arts. The imminent collapse of the American public school system is a tribute to the success of television as an alternate school.

To conclude this overview, let me state that the mafia principle is a work of ontology. Accordingly, in keeping with the practices of eminent philosophers such as Russell and Descartes, I offer the axiom least subject to doubt and then deduce other axioms. My fundamental axiom (AX) is that the similarities between legitimate society and illegitimate society are considerably greater than their dissimilarities. Accordingly, these two sub-societies cannot be defined as x and y, but $x + y_a$ and $y + x_a$. Accordingly, we can first infer that the greater similarities--in a Gresham's law of money applied to societal values--tend to drive out the dissimilarities (AX1). Second, by virtue of the same effect of a greater mass, the leveling down occurs at a faster rate than the leveling up (AX2). Third, in order to save face, the legitimate society must employ an increasing amount of duplicity (AX3).

Moreover, one can subsume other axioms from such basic principles. Thus, the use of chicanery in LME is commendable to the degree that it achieves a desired result ($AX3_a$). LME becomes more crooked as IME becomes less crooked ($AX2_a$). Imbecility rises with the increase in the educational level ($AX1_a$). This phenomenon occurs as the population that rises from the ranks of IME succumbs to the alternate educational system of LME and trades native intelligence for functional illiteracy.

Happily, these axioms compel greater precision in evaluating the behavior of social groups in society. One can, for instance, construct a score card listing criteria such as self-interest without concern for the consequences on others. For such a criterion corporate Wasps would rate high and Italian-Americans low. On the criterion of committing violence on consumers, corporate Wasps would also rate high and Italian-American crooks low.

In the chapters following, these axioms and their usefulness in evaluating performance are extensively illustrated by a more detailed description of the society's institutions and social groups.

Chapter 3

Converting Culture Into a Racket

As society produces a mass man, the legitimate mafia economy and the illegitimate mafia economy become increasingly indistinguishable. Comfortable with his vulgarities and with his subjugation to his management by LME, the mass man sets the cultural standards of the society. The chapter that follows presents this notion of cultural leveling as an affirmation of the mafia principle.

Americans lead the world in consumption. Correspondingly, they are also the world's champion polluters. For years, they have used air and waterways as garbage receptacles. Now, like the Sicilian _mafioso_ who dared to spit at heaven, they get it right back. Even using the ocean has its limitations. Close to land, waste causes pollution. Far at sea, low temperatures and low oxygen preserve wastes in a state of refrigeration. Were a tidal wave suddenly to stir the ocean bottom, New York intellectuals could get seventy years of wastes back in their faces. _Alla faccia tua._

These wastes are the end product of consumption on a heroic scale. In an act of veneration, the suburban wife turns her visit to shops into a ritual. She does not necessarily buy, but seeing all the goodies that could be purchased comforts her spirit. On Saturdays, she is joined by her husband, who spends more of his time in the hardware and sporting goods departments. Her favorite shopping center on one Saturday features a five percent price cut throughout its stores and a free raffle ticket for an automobile. While waiting for the doors to open, she witnesses a ceremonial baptism: the emptying of car ash trays on the parking lot. A wail of sirens signals the excited men, women, and children to rush into the shops. Over the parking area floats a pink balloon with the inscription: "BE PATRIOTIC: SPEND FOR THE GROSS NATIONAL PRODUCT." Amplifiers shriek the tune of Yankee Doodle. Within minutes, the first wave of enraptured spenders pours out of the stores, hauling clothing, toys, jewelry, color television sets, shoes, cosmetics, hardware, sporting goods, cameras, and an assortment of exotic merchandise. A young man blasts through the incoming waves with the first of ten raffled autos a Ford Jet Stream Super 400. The crowd scatters successfully, with the exception of an elderly woman who is mangled beneath the wheels. The Wayne Ambulance Volunteers quietly and efficiently cart her away to a hospital that looks like a summer resort. A New York intellectual with a sign reading: "Keynesian Economics is obsolete" is led through a jeering throng of Republicans by two burly policemen. At the end of a fabulous day, before a background of litter galore, the shopping center's partners divide their earnings: one dollar for you and one for me; two for you and one, two for me.

The sale affirms the society's fine tuning for the making of money. Certain consequences thereby ensue: The relationship between persons is increasingly dominated by pecuniary considerations, with little quarter given to criteria that may result in monetary loss. In addition, the increasing complexity of life issues to a considerable degree from mechanisms geared to making more money or protecting oneself from the pecuniary drive of others. Moreover, the key to fabulous sales is the employment of deception. The technology of ever-better deception outpaces the technology of control of deception. The fastest growing body of technical knowledge in LME is the art of getting someone to do your bidding. Nothing is sacred in the selling of wares. A government report attests to the success with which the patent medicine industry pursues such manipulation. Thanks to this industry, a large segment of the public holds the unverifiable beliefs that a daily dosage of vitamins is indispensable to health and that missing a daily evacuation is courting disaster.

Production and consumption are equalizers in American life. Their effects are uniformly spread through all levels of society. In production, as the hernia rate for the working class falls, the ulcer rate for the managerial class rises. As the working class acquires greater leisure, the governing class spends more time manning the machinery of LME. Managers and workers share the same polluted air. Violence, once confined to working class neighborhoods, moves into fashionable districts. Women are raped without reference to social differences. The rising consumption of cigarettes by women reduces the inequality of the lung cancer rate between the sexes. In volume of sales, men have closed the gap in the scenting of bodies. Males and females become increasingly indistinguishable.

Poisoning, maiming, and killing without discrimination, the motor vehicle is a prime force in cultural leveling and the production of mass man. The automobile is an obscenity hurled at society. It produces more than half the number of disabling accidents, provides lawyers with a substantial income, guarantees undertakers a minimum of fifty thousand funerals annually. The auto mirrors the sanctity bestowed by LME on major contributors to the gross national product. The highway construction it demands, the legal actions it requires, the costs in production and maintenance, provide substantial employment in LME. Wherever the car goes, pressures mount for a hideous collection of gas stations, used car lots, new car lots, junk car lots, car washes, beaneries, mammoth advertising signs readable by functional illiterates at sixty miles per hour, and the finishing touch: a generous sprinkling of trash. Nobody marches against the obscene automobile. Many do against nuclear energy, which, to date, has not produced one fatality.

Americans with a modicum of empathy lose it quickly as they slide under a steering wheel. Give a young male of modest intellect oodles of horsepower and he will use it with lust in his heart. His car becomes a substitute for the manhood society fails to clarify. Ten thousand dollars of automobile is more economical than thirty thousand in psychiatric care. He becomes a man when enthroned in two tons of gleaming metal. He sleeps, eats, works, makes love, and dies in it like a dog. For his immortality and the ecological crisis, he should be buried in it. His car is the offspring of frivolous marketeers and emasculated engineers.

Should American civilization vanish, the automobile will have played a major role. In addition to its disadvantages of pollution, noise, and spreading ugliness, scientists assert that the motor vehicle demonstrates an ability to generate mental pollution by destroying the compassion of people for each other. One can imagine the demise of organized society. All of erstwhile America the beautiful will have been converted into highways and, at strategic points along their course, consumption centers. Cars will be locked in a final love grip, bumper to bumper. Then the rumor will spread that the outstanding engineering contribution to highway esthetics, the mercury vapor lamp, shining on expressionless faces, is causing galloping cancer.

The consumption rat race triggers expenditures in the hundreds of billions of dollars to relieve its consequences. Human beings become phantoms indistinguishable from their surroundings. They are smothered by the meaninglessness of their affluence. They do not approach each other in a friendly spirit. Instead, they are indifferent, fearful, cruel. Ironically, they are not conscious of the image they convey. Their lives are a series of tasks in production and consumption whose major reward is boredom. What is done naturally in backward societies-- going to sleep, digesting food, experiencing tranquility--is facilitated in LME by the use of drugs. Their habitual use is a national pastime catered to by the biggest drug pushers in society: advertisers and salesmen of LME. Another form of escapism, alcohol drinking, generates ten million addicts. These outlays are a measure of self-destruction. The goods of LME are legitimate; those of IME are illegitimate. Other than questions of law, the differences are minor.

At the threshold of this philosophy that everybody is as good as everybody else is license, and beyond--ugliness and violence. Greenwich Village in the City of New York provides an example. Formerly attractive by its authenticity as an Italian enclave, the village is now heavily populated by the let-it-all-hang-out set. Its largest parish, Our Lady of Pompei, reports that its confessionals are used for defecation. In the City of Philadelphia, young adolescents, mostly black males, are converting the city with their graffiti into what appears to be a vast privy house. The liberal-minded hesitate to rebuke out of fear of suppressing freedom and talent. There has not issued to date from the ranks of the muralists one Raffaello.

A similar leveling takes place in religion. Catholics are busy protestantizing their religion. Anyone raising these days the issue of the Virgin Mary would be hustled away as a crank. The halleluiahs that bounce off the walls of a Catholic prayer meeting would outnumber those floated from a Baptist church in the deep South. A story, probably apochryphal but nevertheless suggesting a trend, relates the spirit of homogenization among Protestants, Catholics, and Jews in agreeing on a common house of prayer. After extended talks between representatives of the two Christian religions, the name of the Catholic church was changed from our Lady of Miracles to Saint John the Baptist. After ensuing three-party negotiations, a new name was agreed upon: Yahweh and Son.

The churches no longer foster noble conduct; they have lost their moral hold on the mass man. The assumption of responsibility by the state for implementing moral standards shifts ethical choice from an act of individual conscience to one of political judgment of its consequences. The courts contribute to the neutralization of religion by raising the issue of separation of Church and State. And politicians relegate religion to the last sentence of their speeches, invoking God to support their objectives. Watered down religion gives greater thrust to LME. American protestantism has a shaky foundation anyway: the sexual pathologies of a British king and the constipated bowels of a German. Its ideology was readily converted into the amassing of wealth without acquisition of a guilty conscience. It is now nothing more than a vehicle for generating good feeling. Taking religion seriously would produce chaotic results for LME.

LME converts humans into abstractions for the purpose of their efficient control. A person becomes a series of numbers each of which elicits a coded response. Those aspects of the individual that are computerizable are relevant; the rest are not. He becomes managed in this fashion as a producer, consumer, and citizen, and when the manipulators persuade him to buy goods he does not need and cannot afford, he is dunned as an abstraction. His behavior is expected to be consistent with the computerized judgment made of him; he must so perform to fit LME's needs.

Computerization of human beings provides bureaucrats with opportunities for growth. They weave a network of detail in which the individual becomes trapped. And they possess fertile minds with which to make the complexity greater. The individual tilts with the Internal Revenue Service, the bank, credit agencies, the traffic court, servicemen to keep his goods in repair. He clears up outstanding bills and plunges into more work in order to arrest their accumulation. If he manages to maintain his sanity and keeps the chores of daily living within manageable bounds, he searches for life's meaning in tense metropolitan areas. At times he gives up and seeks refuge in the stupor of alcohol and drugs.

Evasiveness characterizes the bureaucratic response of LME. It marks the triumph of bull over substance. The following letters exemplify this thesis:

> We would be pleased to give every consideration to your request for a grant. Quite candidly, balancing the overwhelming backlog of pending appeals against reduced prospective resources, there is little likelihood of our participation. This does not reflect disinterest in your program so much as comment upon the difficulties of administering finite funds. Although a more positive response is not possible, hopefully you can appreciate our position. Thank you for writing, and may others not so fully committed be encouraged to provide desired support.

> Thank you for bringing to our attention the unpleasant experience associated with the Holiday Inn (no place to sleep at one o'clock in the morning). Please be assured that it is our intent to honor all reservations. We believe that such commitments are carried out over ninety-nine percent of the time. There is always inconvenience when one or more reasons prevent a person from using his intended reservations. We would appreciate another opportunity to restore your confidence in us.

The duty of the purveyors of mass culture in society is to put together a package that titillates the greatest possible number of persons. In literature and in the arts, the focus is on mass marketing of sight, feeling, and sound. A psychology journal has a cover that vies with _Penthouse_. A movie reaches its climax when the principal protagonist lets go a resounding fart. Writers disgorge a stream of sexual fantasies. And by so doing, they acquire a reputation as intellectuals. One writer earns for the nation the notoriety of having nurtured the world's best masturbator. Coarseness and artlessness are chic for the mass man; they gain for LME's managers huge markets. The cult of vulgarity nurtures a generation incapable of drawing a distinction between art and fraud. The cult strips man of his individuality.

The adoration of shock jars the apathetic into experiencing some feeling. LME mass-produces the therapy in the guise of literature and the creative arts. Trade in erotica is a booming business in excess of a billion dollars annually. The right to pornography is an intellectual cause. Tastes divide along social lines. The college educated concentrate on best sellers, nude theater. Those of the working classes focus on hard core pornography. Intellectuals who ignore these distinctions run the risk of becoming declassé. As sales in erotica break records, so does the venereal disease rate. The mass marketing of sex affirms the genius of LME to convert human needs into forms conducive to profit making.

To maximize profits, the managers of taste move from the fanciful to the bizarre and from the bizarre to the fraudulent. The ultimate success of the profit motive will be achieved when man no longer can or wants to discern the truth. In such a regimen of instantly concocted sensation, the last scene will be one in which artist and mass consumer will be locked in an embrace of equality. A few serious artists are genuinely interested in testing the barriers between audience and artifact. The many, however, are solely concerned with the marketing of ego gratification to gullible audiences who have been brainwashed into distrusting their most sensitive impulses. The true name for the Emperor's new clothes is naked avarice and barbarism.

In the economics of advertising for the managers of LME, those buying appetites must be developed that maximize the market at the lowest average cost for the advertising. To achieve this goal, the media amuse, and, in so doing, collect a public for delivery to the advertiser. Whether in the form of broadcast shows or news, the offering must be sufficiently entertaining to dispose the public favorably toward the advertising message. Even the delivery of information must entertain. The size of the managed audience, not art or precision, is the measure of a successful performance. This criterion sacrifices the discerning in order to cultivate and cater to the mass man.

Accordingly, cultural standards are not set by elites, as in the days before the rise of the modern mafia. They are instead fixed by persons with a flair for attracting a large audience. The purveyor of culture is not a Lorenzo de Medici but a Johnny Carson. In contemplating the crowd of semiliterates spawned by the public schools, these managers meet the challenge successfully. Hence the anomaly of a country with increasing educational expenditures and an ever-widening cultural wasteland. The results are a tribute to the media racketeers who succeed in packaging a culture that pays off handsome profits. In their advertising, horses, deodorants, and stubble preoccupy the male; laundry stains, iron in the blood, and constipation the female. Pepsi Cola brings the sexes together in a romp of joy.

Assisted by television, the urban public schools perform yeoman-like service in the leveling process. Out of frustration, its teachers adopt standards that match the rising illiteracy of their students. They give up teaching students how to read and write. The students write with little sense of order and continuity. Their prose sounds like the sharp staccato of television commercials. The mass who cannot think sets the standard for everybody else. A crowd of increasing numbers incapable of thinking provides grist for LME's advertising machine. It was not always this way—at least not in New York City. Jewish teachers used to pump Shakespeare into High School students until they could recite an entire page at a nod. Now, psychological theory is mustered to support the rationalization that memorizing lacks relevance. At the City College of New York, the students used to join in inviting Jascha Heifetz to play in the Great Hall. A D in Freshman mathematics was a respectable grade. Now, when a C is regarded as a disgrace, City College of New York is a school of equal opportunity graduating functional illiterates.

These polyglot cities foster a cult of mediocrity. They operate on the basis of a trading relationship between its cultural groups and public officials. As in traditional Sicily, underlying the human relationships of the urban metropolis is a philosophy of exchange of favors. The citizen views favors given to well-placed persons as bank credit to be called in during some future need. From time to time, he draws his credit in order to obtain favors. He discharges this function in a way that maintains his influence. As in the old country across the sea, this mafia mentality establishes a network of connections with which to trade in accounts. Trading, and not the pursuit of noble ideas, is the essence of the political relationship. A major consequence of such a style of relationship is an equality of mediocrity.

The impulse behind such urban action is what one can acquire with a minimum of personal outlay and what one can get away with. Absence of civic consciousness makes it easier to exercise predatory actions outside the circle of one's relatives and friends. The public official who presides over this human relationship is strictly a political animal. He is for a course of action if such pursuit promotes his interests; and he is blind and deaf to proposals that do not. He serves a civilizing function to the extent that he keeps greed and envy within bounds. But he also makes a noteworthy contribution to the leveling effect.

In this mafia trading system, the law is not a symbol of restraint uniformly applicable to everyone. Instead, the law manifests at a given moment which groups have acquired an exploitive advantage over others. The purpose of law is not the pursuit of justice but the acquisition of advantage. But those on top do not maintain their favorable position indefinitely. As long as one has money, he can hire clever lawyers to upset the power balance. This management of law in LME acts as a machine in perpetual motion that provides full employment to attorneys. The process of law is one which initially exploits power differences, and by narrowing them, contributes to the homogenization of the American.

A question surely comes to mind: do not the rewards and punishments meted out by LME suggest in fact the operation of some worthy moral principle? How can one defend the notion of a mafia trading system in the light of the fact that some public officials are indicted and hauled off to prison? In response to this question, one must make clear that rewards manifest mafia connection more than they do merit. And punishment evidences not justice triumphing but rotten luck. For example, the person who practices no more than routine corruption may suddenly find corruption redefined by those with a vested interest in such redefinition. Or the falling out of grace may be the result of sloppiness in covering one's traces or the inability to discern at what point one has reached the threshold of tolerable corruption.

These failures provide the chance for other persons in positions of authority to switch on the machinery of punishment. One man's downfall is another man's gain. A miscalculation may cause the ruin of a person of prominence. Then people can vicariously enjoy the process of kicking him on his way down. With vigilance over the gossip in the news, these shifts in the fortunes of the exalted in LME provide the crowd with the pleasure of being mean. But the fallen often do not lose out. They renew operations after a period of penance and write best sellers. Moreover, this mafia system of trading produces mixed results. Its consequences may be corruption and a habit of seeking to avoid abiding by the rules of the game. However, it gives people the means to survive in a society that preaches merit but practices a system of trading.

A society has to make a choice between pursuing a vision of virtue or engaging in a system of trading predicated on the maximizing of numbers. The one needs intensive and genuine communication between individuals. The other encourages managers to indulge in fraudulent communication. The one issues from a consensus arising out of frank communication. The other cannot tolerate a communication of highly tuned feelings; it would only serve to diminish the numbers in the crowd and hence profit. Moreover, like a cultural Gresham's law, the quality of the one is debased by the successful pursuit of the other. To pursue lofty values, the individual in society in a mafia world must organize himself into enclaves that succeed in isolating themselves from the manipulated and manipulating crowd.

Out of such disintegration emerges a system of organized advocacies. In seeking maximum advantage, these advocacies engage in clashes of mass thinking. The common value of each of them is to advance its particular interests at the expense of other groups. Since talent cannot in the long run be denied to newly emerging groups, a result of this mass bargaining is a narrowing of differences between groups. A loss also takes place in individual freedom. This is so because the individual, to assert himself, must attach himself to a mass mind. He has to decide to what extent he wishes to resist the demands of organized advocacies or knuckle under. And since above all he wants security, he is inclined to knuckle under.

Accordingly, the restraint on the individual does not come from the voluntary acceptance of a universal moral norm. The norms that condition behavior issue instead from the individual's astute observation of what he can get away with. His mind does not think in terms of what is good or bad. His acts are matters of convenience rather than conscience. Life's meaning is to keep the organized society off his back. Therefore, he does what he does without conviction. He has no deeply felt beliefs about anything. His ideas are transitory; they are whatever the moment dictates. He is the new mass man who provides excellent fodder for LME's managers. Few escape this subjugation of individuality to the crowd.

From such an egalitarian society emerge two kinds of language. There is the language of the mass mind and there is the one of the individual who seeks to achieve an honest communication with other persons. There is the language of truth and the language of government and corporate propaganda. The problem of the individual is how to curtail the ability of influential men to guide his thoughts and actions through a language that blocks communication.

Moreover, the mass mind is given encouragement by the way, to the point of obsession, the psychology behind events enthralls us. This obsession is disarming; it weakens the will to evaluate events and encourages permissiveness. The psychological dimension becomes the only dimension. Psychology is all. The only meaning is psychic meaning. Life is catalogued rather than evaluated. In this way, an evaluation of LME is discouraged. The people become passive, and their lives are shaped by LME's managers. The language of truth becomes corrupted; for if the truthful wish to be listened to in a society of organized advocacies, they must adopt its language. To maintain their honesty, they must become corrupt.

From these contests between lofty values and the mass man evolves a society of equality under the aegis of an omnipotent state. We can avoid this fate only if somehow each of us helps the other to acts of authenticity and generosity. However, this is unlikely because everybody feels that everybody else is being unfair. Everyone feels that he is knuckling under to the unfair demands of organized advocacies. There is little recognition of a common necessity. There is no empathy; no sense of identification. One's fellow man is a stranger. Selfishness nurtures the omnipotent state.

In such a society of state-managed equality, the managers who direct the society's institutions cannot claim superiority for doing so. The mass man feels that he is as good as anybody else; he is touchy about any suggestion to the contrary; if he is vulgar, he will rebel at being told so. In these circumstances, the influential justify their position of superiority by asserting that they can best serve the interests of the mass man. Whether they actually promote such interests is a different question. Their task is to convince the crowd that they actually do so. They serve the tastes of the crowd and delude themselves into believing they do not.

Accordingly, individuality succumbs in a society of equals. The individual must operate with a crowd--at work, in public places, in political life, at school, in dealing with the bureaucracies, in his leisure activity. He must be disposed to render what would appeal to a crowd. In a society of the average man who rules (or thinks he does) there is little way to assert individuality. The individual becomes unimportant. He cannot impose his own values on the mass man or expect the mass man to assist in their fulfillment. Moreover, if he disassociates from the crowd, nobody, least of all the influential in LME, will give him any attention. If he tries to impose his values on the mass, he may become isolated. The individual is interchangeable and replaceable. His personal feelings and thoughts carry small weight.

Thus the conversion of culture into a racket sets the scene for the debasement of man.

PART TWO: Let's Kiss Hands

Chapter 4

Corporate Hit Men

The corporate man of LME rushes through life wearing a mask and
programming his behavior to meet the exigencies of getting ahead. He
is neither heroic nor cowardly, but shrewd. As a super-salesman,
the slick corporate man acts as a vital cog in the machinery of managed
consumption. Corporate man and spouse are generally registered Republicans. An affiliation with the other party would render them dé-
classé. Of Anglo-Saxon protestant descent in the upper echelons of
the corporate structure, he is threatened by attempts of lesser Americans
to invade his social and economic enclaves. And while he laments the
passing of old American values, his business is a principal vehicle of
their destruction.

His mafia-like qualities include foremost a constant jockeying for
position in the organization in the hope of becoming a capo and assess-
ing who has power and who has not. His measure of success, in government or corporation, is getting to the top of the heap. His loyalty
is not to his organization, from which he freely disassociates should
a better opportunity arise, but to himself. His strongest conviction
is that of himself and he uses the organization for this end. To his
colleagues, corporate man is not an image of craftsmanship but of envy
because of his position in the hierarchy. The successful corporate
man is not viewed as an artist but as a master mafioso. He is envied
not respected. The measure of his worth is something that inheres not
within his individuality but in his position in the organization. With
such kind of achievement, he is a prominent figure; without it he is a
bum.

Corporate man is a masked marketeer changing his personality to
suit his fundamental goal of increasing his market value. He judges
persons by their capacity to further his undisclosed objective. He
speaks for the record, in the interest of serving the function of marketing himself. Accordingly, it is difficult to have an authentic relationship with him; it is difficult to penetrate his soul. He is a
manipulator of relationships for his own advancement. And the system rewards him for his successful manipulations. As an influential
man, he has an impact on the direction that society takes. But he
does not direct society through a vision of human growth. Rather, the

direction he requires to market himself is the direction in which he
steers society.

The willing minion of the system, he moves through life from one
sensation to the next, devoid of historical as well as religious perspective. He concedes that society is in trouble but believes it is the fault
of troublemakers. Not wishing to offend, he is noncommittal, yet he is receptive to supporting the criticism of persons who offend his sensibilities. He is deceived by politicians who do not fully reveal their cards
and by writers who zoom to the top of best seller lists with instant clarification of complex matters. He is adept at making money. Corporate man
is an individual, stout because of excessive eating and little exercise,
at the helm of an aggressive-looking automobile, with an impasssive look
screwed onto his face. As super-salesman, he sustains the machinery of
LME.

He struggles to maintain his balance on the treadmill of income, consumption, relief from both through booze and drugs, and more income. He
spends much of his time buying goods, consuming them, paying for them, re-
cuperating from their use. At times, the futility of an ever-rising level
of consumption makes him irritable. A characteristic of IME--doing things
quietly--can be found in the habits of corporate man in LME. In the wintry
dawn of a December morning, for example, curtained limousines quietly pulled
up before the entrance of a secluded mansion. The banking chiefs pouring
out of the mafia-type cars regrouped at the breakfast table of the super
chief. They warned the capo dei capi about the possible disaster attending
the sale of their product. Appropriate decisions were made to keep things
off the record. The chiefs left as discreetly as they had arrived. The
chiefs were senior executives of banks and brokerage houses. The chief of
chiefs was the mayor of New York City.

Corporate man is so busy making transactions that he does not have
the time to think of where he came from and where he is headed. He cannot
face death realistically; humans do not die, but "pass away". His major
preoccupations, judging from his conversations, are babes, booze, baseball,
and bullion. Food, television, cars, and orgasms round out the good life.
He is trained to respond dutifully to planned obsolescence, consistent with
the philosophy of a former board chairman of the General Motors Corporation
who stated that planned obsolescence means progress. He sustains the sys-
em's need for the proliferation of goods which now include powered back-
scratchers, pink cigarettes for weddings and blue for bar mitzvahs, and
Cupid's Quiver liquid douche concentrates in floral scents (orange, blossom,
and jasmine). For corporate man, the great society consists of a third
scoop of ice cream, a guarantee against not having to leave childhood for
the rigors of adult life. Under corporate direction, nirvana comes when
American man becomes well-fed, well-clothed, well-housed, and well-
titillated. Mechanized pleasure is LME's ethic; corporate man is tuned
into an erotic utopia that make him impatient with fine judgment.

In the upper layers of the corporate class, one finds Wasp preservers of the traditional American faith. Armed with money and connections, they select those Americans who support old time religion in a manner worthy of immortality in stone. On a hill at Valley Forge they have listed in granite the seventeen political and economic rights of Americans, which protect the dignity and freedom of the individual. The corporation in which they place their investments has destroyed many of these freedoms. These preservers of the faith fancy themselves self-made men in contrast with present-day ethnics. Preacher Billy Graham states:

> We also wrestled with poverty except we did
> not know we were poor. We did not have sociolo-
> gists, educators, and newscasters constantly re-
> minding us of how poor we were. We also had the
> problem of rats. The only difference between
> then and now is we did not call upon the govern-
> ment to kill them. We killed our own. 1.

Corporate man's gypsy life dutifully following the orders of his firm allows suburban governments to operate as private clubs serving the interests of builders and land speculators. Together with the highway consortium, these groups are a private circle within government, destroying what first attracted people to the suburbs in the beginning. Suburban corporate man runs up the flag on a holiday, and then spends time on chores such as shining the car or mowing the grass, and in pleasure pursuits such as cocktail and dinner parties or a swim at the club. The next morning he brings down the flag (sensitive to the ritual prescribed by custom) and then ventures forth to make a killing in sales. His wife looks upon feminist organizations such as NOW as "way out". The opportunity for venting milder forms of male envy is found within the preferred League of Women Voters. The Gung-ho types in the League channel their neuroticisms into service of country through an exercise of organized superficiality. For the wife who considers the League too risky, there are many social affairs that regularly make the suburban society page. She is photographed at a charity ball, horse show, beside a horse, grasping a cocktail, holding a silver cup.

In a Philadelphia suburban community, the preponderant majority of the corporate men automatically reach for the Republican master lever. The Republican primary is in effect the election. In one for the school board, the incumbent came out in support of quality education, a move calculated to gain the support of fellow Republicans who believe in orderly progress; a woman candidate placed her sex on the line; a third candidate

---

1. The Philadelphia Evening Bulletin, October 16, 1971.

presented as his platform his happy public school children; and a fourth, a college professor, foolishly addressed the issues. The first three candidates won handsomely.

The profit motive shapes the physical contours of this community. Twenty-five gas stations line a two-mile stretch of highway, which amounts roughly to one every five hundred linear feet. In a court suit brought by the Gulf Oil Corporation, owners of five of the stations, the courts stated that the community could not control their number. In effect, the criterion stipulated by the judge was the ability of the firm to make a profit. Dispersed among the gasoline stations are hamburger joints, including Gino's, McDonalds, and Burger King. The shopping centers and auto dealerships complete the scene on a stretch of road that once was among the most attractive in the nation. The commercial strip is a constant threat of spreading ugliness. Its free-standing advertising signs resemble the gods of industry perched on pedestals.

A believer in the private enterprise system, corporate man hesitates to protest this spreading vulgarity. The courts join this alliance for progress by taking the view that local government can concern itself only with the health, safety, and morals of the public and not with its esthetic requirements. The government is manipulated by developers who manage to obtain political decisions that conflict with the community's well-being. Politicians count on the apathy of corporate man and resent the sporadic intervention of the community's residents. The stakes are high. An investment can be quadrupled overnight by getting a change in zoning after the purchase of land.

This land speculation with the connivance of public officials has been going on ever since the British kings gave out parcels to their bosom pals.

> When the Duke of York received the grant,
> he separated them and divided the least of the
> two, called New Jersey, between two of his
> favourites, Carteret and Berkley, the first of
> whom had received the eastern and the other the
> western part of the province, who had solicited
> this vast territory with no other view but to
> put it up for sale. Several adventurers bought
> large districts of them at a low price, which
> they then divided and sold again in smaller
> parcels.   2.

---

2. Abbé Raynal. Philosophical and Political History of the British Settlements and Trade in North America, Edinburgh, Scotland: C. Denovan 1779, p. 87.

In the same suburban community, a builder bought a piece of land for thirty-five thousand dollars, ran successfully for the township board of commissioners, persuaded his colleagues to rezone, and then sold it for eight hundred thousand dollars. In a community nearby, a clever lawyer bought a house from a black woman for five hundred dollars, turned around and sold it to a new housing authority for thirty-five thousand dollars. In its elections for local government, support from the Republican party machine is tantamount to winning office. A product of such control is a disease that often afflicts the offspring of marriages between first cousins. A challenger to the chosen candidate of the machine needs considerable sums of money to pose a serious challenge. One such person, loaded with money and advertising techniques offered his classical name, his fertility, and his belief in quality education as inducements to vote for him. He plastered his name on every utility pole and traffic sign in the community. Pictures of his ample family appeared in the local press. His radio commercial repeated his name to a backdrop of muffled tympani. Hamilton won by a whisker.

The members of his community cannot escape progress. Highways, jet planes, and commercial strips pursue them should they try to flee. Zoning ordinances they believed would guarantee them quality living are easily subverted with money, sharp lawyers, and political connections. The engineers who could provide counsel to the community are employed by vested interests and are therefore reluctant to say anything that might jeopardize their jobs. Those affiliated with universities also hesitate to provide technical assistance to members of the community because of their connections with government and business.

This circus is costly to the taxpayer. With a population of thirty thousand, the taxpayers of the community feed a mafia clique of about a hundred and fifty full-time civil servants. The budget, excluding school costs, amounts to over two million dollars. With salaries comparable to those of the City of Philadelphia, a quarter of the budget goes to a police department of fifty men, whose primary duties include controlling traffic and running down complaints of women irritated by children and dogs. The operation is listed in the budget as police protection. One officer, at a salary of eighteen thousand dollars, works full time in the construction business. At times, boredom provokes the police to indulge in petty harassment. To avoid the disabilities that may occur from overwork, the township employees enjoy a thirty-seven hour work week, four weeks' vacation with pay, and thirteen paid holidays each year. Adding a school budget of about eight million dollars, the local government costs amount to about four hundred dollars for each man, woman, and child in the community. The school board grinds out additional expenditures each year as enrollment declines. Corporate man takes it without a murmur. The little people complain, but they lack the information, money, and organization with which

-55-

to react effectively against the community's mafia cliques. The management principle that best explains these operations in the community is that the amount of money a government needs is a function of its skill in extracting funds from taxpayers.

Ironically, the hippie children of suburbia are often corporate man's offspring. They play a part calling for unconventional regalia and a developed contempt for making money. Their corporate fathers subsidize their liberation. They reject the system of LME but prey on its beneficence. The hippie meets the challenge by squatting, playing the sole chord he knows on the guitar, and moodily contemplating his navel. At times cerebrally underprivileged, he assumes a posture of eastern wisdom to temper his disability. As corporate father dedicates his life to manning the productive machinery of LME, corporate offspring makes a fetish of low productivity. His children wear the paraphernalia of rejection and pursue the inner self. After some perfunctory search, they find little.

The term "hippie," used originally to refer to youth rebelling against society, has lost precision. It now covers a variety of subspecies; gurus, freaks, plastics, loving grass sitters, frisbee specialists, persons with mental disorders of melancholia and violent impulse. Hippies include a formidable contingent united against the exercise of the intellect, on whose festoonery can be emblazoned: SLOBS--Students Lovingly Organized against Brain Stress. They use drugs to escape from themselves and to obtain instant revelation through a quick intoxication in color. By basing their communication on noise, color, pictures, and movement, they transport themselves back to the Stone Age. Their life style is a romp in slow motion like the commercials on television, dictated just as much by LME as that of the corporate man they ridicule. The culture they extol is managed by young exploiters who make the more colorful robber barons in the early days of LME seem like amateurs. Some intellectuals assign to this culture a sublime mission.

This posture against the system is a fragile vestment easily destroyed by predatory humans; a game of narcissism that readily turns into cannibalism; a litany of futile existence. If only these dissidents took up something, even the digging variety of anthropology. These characteristics of corporate child are products of LME. He grows up in a fraudulent environment. He describes a society that does not exist. He finds it difficult to make fine judgments. He is difficult to educate. His supporters are his worst enemies. He is the mirror of a mafia society.

In part, the uneasy relationship between corporate father and corporate son arises from corporate man's demystification. He is increasingly seen by the public as a cautious politician playing his cards close to the chest. He trades candor for money. To make money, he panders to values for which he has contempt; with this ambivalence, he acquires the disrespect of his children. In Roman mythology, Mercury was the God presiding over banking and commerce. He was also the God of Thieves. In the present climate of opinion, it is doubtful if the public would object to lumping together corporate executive and thief.

In theory, corporate men are selected by the stockholders in their organizations. In practice, they belong to a tight, self-perpetuating oligarchy whose membership is influenced by those controlling the flow of money into corporations. The union of corporate managers is not totally closed, however; an outsider can move into the circle if he plays it right and persuades his superiors that he will play it right for them. On the way to the top, a novice of acceptable social background must be ready to move freely between organizations and must convince the top dog that he is one of the lieutenants. While his relationships with subordinates may always be amicable, they are rarely affectionate. But was ever a prince truly loved by his courtiers? He must be conservative in projecting his goals while convincing his loyal soldiers that he is daring. He must dominate forces that pose a threat to his position, forestalling menacing moves from his subordinates and persuading his superiors of his extraordinary abilities. Corporate man is not a monster; indeed, he is often _simpatico_. His failures stem from the role he must play in LME.

His social morality is whatever morality he can get away with in the performance of his corporate role. Commenting on the public disclosure of a firm's secret disbursement of money to politicians one of its executives stated:

> I should have been a lot smarter than I was.
> I kind of fell into what seemed to be the practice of
> the times. I don't know why the company was singled
> out for such publicity. We were not the only ones.
> A large number of companies made illegal corporate
> contributions. I don't know that 3M did anything diff-
> erent than a great many other companies did. 3.

Some corporate gifts have a sentimental quality. Thus, the Gulf Corporation, in a spirit of largesse, gave ten thousand dollars to the executive director of the New Jersey Turnpike Commission. The firm described the gift as a "thank you present."

Accordingly, the relevance of law is not whether it should be obeyed, but whether it serves corporate interests, and when it does not, whether it can be violated with impunity. As a general rule, truth is whatever the corporate organization persuades the public it is. At times, corporate man has to prod the public into the proper consciousness. Unless required by

---

3. The New York Times, March 9, 1975, Business Section, page 16.

law to do so, the corporation must not inform the public about the consequences of consuming its product.

The attorneys who counsel corporate men set the tone of exploitation in LME. They have converted auto insurance and medical malpractice suits into lucrative rackets. Auto no-fault, defended by proponents on the basis that it would decrease the number of lawsuits, has increased them; clever lawyers inflate injuries over the threshold to introduce them into court proceedings. Another source of income, bankruptcy proceedings, are a bonanza. In the first year of litigation in the W. T. Grant Company bankruptcy, legal services cost six million dollars. In LME generally, the amount of money spent in legal fees doubles each decade. There are also sharp lawyers among the society's ethnic groups. But their surnames reveal their inferior caste. They are out on the street. The Brahmin attorneys operate less obtrusively within the recesses of government and corporation.

The executives in these corporations are judged according to economic criteria such as profit, production, and efficiency. At times, judgment of whether a corporate man is a good or bad company man rests on intangible factors that make him feel insecure and impel him to put on a show of loyalty for the capo. His organization, moreover, must develop a strategy; it cannot lead a life of improvisation. A plan is a calculated hope, a compromise of various viewpoints advanced by different units in the organization. The plan is successful if the corporate manager can hide his tactics in prodding his lieutenants toward the outcome he desires. In such maneuvering, he has the advantage of surprise and the power of punishment. He also can use the ambition of his subordinates as a tool. Ambition makes corporate men easy to manipulate.

Like government and university, their corporation cannot move toward a vision of excellence. Myriad demands are made on the organization by government, labor unions, environmentalists, consumers, church groups, all of which tend to erode corporate autonomy. In no small measure, the increasingly litigious relationship of the society's members contributes to this erosion. Whereas settlements would formerly be made face to face by laymen, organizations increasingly resort to litigation in their dealings with each other. The law has become the court of first resort. A consequence of this relentless barrage of litigation is corporate adoption of a mafia characteristic: trying to do things quietly. Another effect is that organization decisions are neither extraordinarily good nor bad. Internally, the conflicting purposes of a corporation's different lieutenants have similar results.

At times, the desire of these firms to feel the pulse of the outer society promotes self-deception. Executives shop around for the right university professor to assist them in the collection of desired information. Mindful not to bite the hand that feeds them, some scholars serve up information that will not be unduly offensive to their patrons. Accordingly, the information they avowedly seek from the base of society is tainted.

The national legislature and the courts have encouraged this political consciousness. The Congress has legalized the creation of political organizations by corporations. The Supreme Court has ruled that the State of Massachusetts cannot forbid corporations to lobby voters during a referendum on the income tax. The Court saw no importance in the capacity of a big corporation to exert a profound influence on opinion by virtue of the resources it can command. A corporation can saturate news channels, but the individual lacks the means with which to respond effectively. In a masterpiece of rationalization, the Court stated that such a prohibition on the corporation limits its first amendment rights. Thus, the rights given the individual by the constitution are bestowed upon the corporation. A legal fiction created by the state is given the right to devour the individual it is supposed to serve. It is like a Frankenstein monster that, once created, overpowers its creator.

The corporate manager must make decisions in a way that, hopefully, subordinates department heads to his will. The relative influence of different departments reflects the chief executive's judgment about the contribution of each to the mission of the organization. Unruly subordinates require delicate handling. Thus, the manager can make it difficult for a subordinate through budget allocations, subtle curtailment of the prerogatives of office, or assignment of tasks so difficult as to make their accomplishment unlikely. In performing distasteful but necessary tasks, the corporate managers must at the same time gain the confidence of the subordinate's constituency. They can undermine the position of subordinates by lunching with constituents in a spirit of good fellowship or by announcing an open door policy. In short, the corporate manager can be devious but not heavy-handed. Obstructionists must be eliminated with a certain delicacy. The manager must keep in mind that he operates a loosely integrated collection of semi-independent duchies whose chiefs guard their respective territories and resent the intrusion of an outsider, including the chief executive himself. While these tactics of the corporate manager are relatively more delicate, they do not differ fundamentally from those of managers in IME.

In after-dinner speeches and at stockholder meetings, corporate men like to talk about their social responsibilities. It is not clear whether their avowals to do more social acts issue from moral perturbations or from tactical maneuvers calculated to ease pressures generated from outside the corporation. The corporate men who indulge in such talk are often damned when they do and damned when they don't. The criticism comes from economists, who, starting from questionable premises about LME, conclude with unimpeachable logic that it is not the function of a manager to be responsible. At the other extreme are institutionalists who assert the contrary and who are skeptical about the sincerity behind corporate statements on social responsibility. One must therefore turn to the institutional constraints under which corporate men labor to discern the realities.

As per capita income rises, an increasing margin of goods has to be sold by corporate man on the basis of hoodwinking consumers into believing they need what they did not want before the hoodwinking began. The margin has reached considerable proportions. If Americans suddenly no longer read billboards, no longer listened to the radio or watched television, succeeded in keeping salesmen off the telephone and the property, no longer read their junk mail, the effect on the economy would be disastrous. Such disaster is avoided by making the individual a tool of LME.

Corporate man has to generate insecurities that drive individuals to sales counters. He does this through advertising that reaches the brink of falsehood without actually falling in. The few convince the many to do what is good for LME. The control of tastes is motivated neither by the desire to promote the social welfare nor by the intent to sharpen the consumer's perceptions. The advertising pitch is based on the assumption that the consumer is not especially bright. This style of persuasion has been so successful that it is even used profitably in merchandising candidates for United States President.

A producer who succeeds in developing a substantial demand for a product before publicity on its harmful effects mounts threateningly, acquires the power to defend himself against increasing attacks on its use. Thus, cigarette smoking, despite its record of lung cancer, heart disease, chronic bronchitis, and emphysema, manages to hold its own, with the assistance of political lobbying and advertising in the hundreds of millions of dollars. The corporate men who defend cigarette smoking obdurately defend their supporting "research" questioning the scientific methodology of associating cigarette smoking with disease. At the same time, they readily accept studies associating cigarette sales with advertising expenditure. With the similar respect for making money, the consumption of alcohol, with its record of crime, disease, and half the annual deaths on the highways, is managed diffidently. By contrast, the smoking of marijuana commands a substantial amount of resources against it. One is therefore drawn to the conclusion that the extent of corporate man's social responsibilities is related to his power to ignore them.

The universal theme of advertising is an optimistic belief that a small outlay of money will catapult a person from utter despair to bliss. Advertising has nurtured instant success industries including weight watching, sex technique improvement, dieting that makes you eat as much as you want, relaxation without a minimum of effort, and exercise that can be performed while relaxing on a couch. A relatively inexpensive item such as a deodorant, a pill, a cigarillo, an antiseptic mouth wash, or a laxative will convert a mini-person into a conqueror. The drug industry spends over two hundred million dollars annually advertising its wares on television. Their commercials create a sense of insecurity in the viewer and then advise what drug can be taken to alleviate it. It is difficult to state whether such advertising reflects American culture or whether the system shapes the culture. In any case, the manner in which Americans tolerate, if not enjoy, listening in song to praise of chewing gum that does not stick to false teeth surely must have profound meaning. The way in which television commercials radiate happiness and beauty in a world of frustration and ugliness is worthy at least of some sociological study. If a visitor from outerterrestrial space were to visit the United States and try to deduce the character of its people from commercials, he might conclude that the land was populated by buffoons.

Nothing is sacred for corporate man's advertisers, not even a bowel movement. LME's university apologists for advertising state that it keeps prices down, reduces the cost of research, and increases the competitiveness of the market. These beneficent results can be granted. But the social and esthetic consequences of advertising include deception, manipulation, and bad taste. The general rule of advertising is that if the ad sells goods, it's OK. Questions of taste are irrelevant. Thus, a billboard shows the rear view of a woman in tight jeans with an announcement across ample buttocks stating: He who loves me follows me--Jesus Jeans. Mr. Adelstein, the clever young man marketing the jeans, in his complaint about the hostile reaction, protests that Jesus is just a name. In the age before the rise of LME, men of intelligence in the upper social class used their brains to develop the arts. In these days, their descendants use their talent to manipulate the crowd into buying.

The cultural varieties of advertising are attested by the following ditty in the London subway:

> Erminrude, my Erminrude
> My softly cooing dove,
> when shall we be joined
> in everlasting love?
>
> Archibald, dear Archibald,
> I've only this to say:
> Take me first to Barrington's
> And you can name the day.

These corporate persuasions to buy disturb economists. Their discipline is grounded on the assumption that the economic system is ordered by individual preferences expressed by consumer choices in a competitive market. The consumer is king. He expresses his preferences for products at particular prices and he gets what he wants. It is therefore embarrassing to adhere to a premise that brings one to the conclusion that the welfare of the consumer is promoted by poisoning, maiming, and killing him. Economists have placed the notion of consumer preference in such convenient analytical use that they are reluctant to yield to the facts. If the assumption of consumer preference were discarded, sophomore economics would be reduced to a chaotic state. But the managers of LME use this very economics to defend the system and shape public policy.

Advertising has been perfected to the point where it can thwart the application of reason to choice and blur the esthetic sense. That is how it has to be, however, for if advertising were to adopt standards of reason and esthetic judgment, it would no longer be advertising. If the purpose of advertising is to fill the public's needs for information, the rational course of action would be to support institutions that would better serve such a function. If the objective of advertising is to deceive, the public (if it were rational) would demand that the deception be stopped. In either case, the advertising would cease.

> To assert aesthetic goals is also to interfere seriously with the management of the consumer. This, in many of its manifestations, requires dissonance--a jarring of the aesthetic sensibilities. This jarring effect then becomes competitive. The same principles of planned dissonance are even more spectacularly in evidence in the radio and on television. They also characterize the design or packaging of numerous industrial products. An effort is made to bring this dissonance within the ambit of social goals. It is defended interestingly by the contention that it "gives the consumer what he wants." If he did not approve, he would not respond. A man who comes to a full stop because he is hit over the head with an ax proves similarly by his response that it was what he was yearning for. 1.

Even the most ardent believer in consumer sovereignty would concede that consumers need a little prodding. It must be granted also that the deception reflects a measure of the public's tolerance for it. If television producers can interrupt a movie with thirty commercials in the course of an hour and get away with it, cultural democracy is at work. It is difficult to label one factor cause and the other effect. Moreover, the deception goes on despite government regulation. Being caught in a lie is solved by moving to another. This provides continuous employment for bureaucrats--an additional worthy consequence of advertising.

---

1. John K. Galbraith. The Industrial State, p. 348-49.

Therefore, the argument about whether producer sovereignty or consumer sovereignty prevails in LME raises a false dilemma. Either notion is much too neat, reflecting more the politics of academic debate than the demands of reality. The producer in LME does not enjoy sovereign power like that of a Louis XIV. He must manipulate the consumer and work at it continually. He must establish an association between his product and the quest for status and pleasure. Having done so, he must maintain this association by indicating the deprivation that would ensue if the product were not consumed. He must belt the psyche of the consumer hard and repeatedly until he succeeds in obtaining a Pavlovian response. His task is made easier by the constant pressure of the mass media to buy goods. A forced choice of producer or consumer sovereignty would obscure this interplay. The consequences, moreover, of this producer-consumer relationship are unpredictable. Some advertising campaigns succeed and some fail. Their fate at times is determined by a transitory mood. The mini-maxi revolution of the 1960's is a case in point. Who, for example, would have dared to predict that young women would dress to just below their buttocks on the inside and to their ankles on the outside?

Peter Drucker, a man of considerable reputation, suggests that consumer values and expectations are given and that the role of the firm is to develop a marketing strategy that ties its products to these values and expectations.

> As long as one thinks of "our product", one is still thinking in terms of selling rather than in terms of marketing. What matters is the customer's behavior, his values, and his expectations. And under this aspect, one's own business, let alone one's own product, hardly exists at all. In a true marketing point of view no product and no company is assumed to have the slightest importance to the customer or indeed to be even noticed by him. It is axiomatic that the customer is only interested in the satisfaction he seeks and in his needs and expectations. The customer's question is always: What will this product or this business do for me tomorrow?

> It is for instance not true that the American automobile industry has not been safety-conscious. On the contrary, it pioneered in safe-driving instruction and in the design of safe highways. It did a great deal to reduce the frequency of accidents--and with considerable success. What it is penalized for today, however, is its failure to make an accident itself less dangerous. Yet when the manufacturers tried to introduce safety-engineered cars, the public refused to buy them. 2.

---

2. Peter F. Drucker. The Age of Discontinuity, New York: Harper and Row, 1968.

Mr. Drucker assumes consumer values as given. He misses the point on
the so-called safety-engineered cars. After fifty years of brainwashing,
bumperless cars and aircraft carrier fenders were inevitable. His analysis is more an article of faith pleasing to the managers of LME. Consumer sovereignty is fairly accurate in describing the purchase of a
bunch of carrots and inadequate in interpreting the sale of an automobile. 3 .

The mass media are a vital arm in directing consumer sovereignty in
the right direction. The racket objective of the mass media is capturing an audience for their advertisers. the goal corrupts the information they convey. As the size-of-audience objective rises, the accuracy
of the information becomes more diluted. The blandishments with which
the media's managers dress the information become more important than
the information itself. Each mass of detail drawn together by day, by
week, by month is entertaining but soon forgotten. But such forgetful-
ness is insignificant so long as the individual remains hooked to the
racket objective. The media's managers perform in such fashion not because of malevolence but because they need to capture particular audiences. They structure a given public's source of information. The
thrust of the media is not to encourage a dialogue in the interest of
rational decisions, but to sensationalize in order to entertain and
keep hooked a particular segment of society. The society's members do
not interact through the media, as a substitute for the traditional
act of politics, so much as they choose the vehicle that approximates
their bias. In this way, the media foster fantasy and isolation. They
have the most glorious racket of them all; for while they pursue their
profit-making objective, they claim to champion freedom of communication. The freedom redounds not to the public, but to the media's managers, who define reality and set the public agenda.

Like the media, the peccadilloes of corporate man are managed by
the society in more gentle fashion than those committed by members of
IME. The Penn Central Railroad, for example, was one of the most imaginative of conglomerates. Its managers built an empire that ran from
hotels to clothing plants, while purportedly minding the railroad. Its
merger with the New York Central was approved by the Interstate Commerce
Commission of the national government and supported by the business community as an earnest of lower costs and improved service. Not too long there-

---

3. Marshall's concept of demand, a substantial part of the foundation of
economics, is carrot-oriented. The automobile offers a complex bundle of
satisfactions compared to carrots. Lawrence Abbott has tried to revise
the theory of the firm to allow for this evolution of consumption. It is
a tribute to the tenacity of the economics profession that Marshall is
more revered for the elegance of his analysis than is Abbott for his realism.

after, the empire collapsed. Some of the details border on the romantic.
In a deal involving investment in an air carrier, the conglomerate was
taken for four million dollars by a Bavarian financier brooding over his
losses in the carrier. His grab was consummated in the following way.
Two lawyers, both with court records but impeccable educational back-
grounds and connections in the national government, arranged a loan for
Penn Central and placed the funds in a Lichtenstein bank. The firm gave
the sulking yodeler from Bavaria loan privileges against the bank deposit,
which he claimed up to the full amount of the loan. One of the lawyers,
Francis Rosenbaum, who later received a light jail sentence for swindling
the United States Navy, was permitted visits to his villa in Virginia.
His accomplice drew interest on the money for two years. The executives
of the Penn Central sold their shares of the firm's stock just before the
securities plummeted in value on the stock exchange. Twenty days before
bankruptcy, the firm paid three quarters of a million dollars in salary
increases to its executives. The chief executive officer insured himself
against liability for improper conduct. None of the corporate men in the
conglomerate were ever indicted.

William J. Ronan, a transportation specialist, received a gift of
three quarters of a million dollars from former Vice President Nelson
Rockefeller. He failed to disclose the gift at the time of his appointment as chairman of the Port Authority of New York and New Jersey. A
special legislative committee of the State of New Jersey, in a demonstra-
tion of what comprises morality in LME, concluded that the gift was not
illegal and hence unworthy of a course of action against Mr. Ronan.

The public record indicates that some twenty-five of the biggest
corporations in LME have used secret funds with which to bribe domestic
and foreign public officials. It takes these firms about five seconds
of operations to pay the penalties imposed on them for these dealings.
Paying the penalties is like taking out a license to bribe. In another
example of corporate-government morality, in August of 1971, the antitrust division of the United States Department of Justice announced it
was abandoning its prosecution of three antitrust suits against a conglomerate, the International Telephone and Telegraph Company. Rumor
linked the decision to a commitment by the firm to contribute half a
million dollars toward the Republican National Convention. With annual
sales in excess of seven billion dollars, the communications firm at
that time was also in the hotel, car rental, insurance, and baking business. In the prior decade, the International Telephone and Telegraph
Company had swallowed up about a hundred firms. Four months prior to
the announced settlement, the antitrust chief went on record as strongly
favoring a court suit to determine whether existing law would be

applicable in controlling the wave of conglomerate mergers. Shortly thereafter, the antitrust chief changed his mind and so informed the Deputy Attorney General. An agreement between the firm and the government was reached, settling the suit out of court. Following the settlement, the antitrust chief was appointed a federal judge.

Chapter 5

The Kiss of Death

The government of LME is not a distinct and separate institution. Indeed, it is so intertwined with business that often the difference between public and corporate official is difficult to discern. While they may appear at times as adversaries, their relationship tends to be cozy. The corporate officials of big firms may grumble in the course of negotiating with the government, but in the long run they get their way. The occasional quarrels between government and business reflect often periodic changes in the rules of their marriage. Accordingly, discussing government and corporation separately is only a matter of convenience.

American government has undergone profound change. If a young person at the end of the second World War had been told that in the name of freedom his government would soon become a subverter of governments; would condone political assassination; would spy on, bug, and wiretap its own people; would subvert American institutions; that its presidents would start their own private wars and defend them with Machiavellian tactics, he would have been incredulous. The American government began its history two hundred years ago without princes, without a military machine, without an established religion, and without a record of oppressing foreigners. Now, its princes of state initiate their own wars, the military establishment operates an inner government, and the state religion is Machiavellismo. Each advancement of its power bestows on freedom the kiss of death.

Fear of communism was an important factor behind this evolution. The astute exploitation of this fear catapulted many politicians to positions of prominence. Politicians described the communist challenge as the expansionist tyranny of international communism without moral principle and without honor. As this conspiracy doctrine gained currency, they structured a government whose conduct resembled that ascribed to the adversary. They left a legacy of government that cannot be trusted.

Government lacks an inherent warrant to coerce individuals into a prescribed course of behavior beyond that necessary to prevent them from harming each other. Government does not exist independent of the individuals it represents. Rationally, individual actions can be curtailed only through

-67-

negotiating a consensus on the extent of the restriction people wish to impose on themselves. Beyond his potential to harm others, the individual should be free to pursue his or her own course of action. He can be asked to exercise greater restraint through an exchange of information and through an appeal to his sense of fairness. The use of government power to exact conduct beyond this minimum social contract encourages employment of power to counter its efforts.

Having acquired an appetite for coercion, government ignores this social limit. Allegedly, its stronger controls promote the common good. To this end, government monitors the thoughts and behavior of the citizenry receiving its beneficence. Functions derive increasingly from coercion and rarely from agreement. The government can rightfully demand only that people not be unduly anti-social. It can require that people be civil and reasonably literate. Logic cannot project these limits further, not even to prescribe the way in which these qualities should be acquired. When government insists its citizens adjust to policies not of their making, it curtails the right of man to be maladjusted.

This official preference for automatic and unquestioned obedience emerges from needs of organization generally. For the orderly maintenance of policy and institutions, people must be manipulated. This universal need for control, as a substitute for participation, for rhetoric rather than truth, for fantasy rather than reality, can be easily ascribed to a cabal of devils. But in fact, their necessity comes from technological imperatives that trap modern society. The manipulating state makes technological commitments that require deception for their orderly evolution. The government cannot rely upon ethical restraints within people. For the sake of maintaining modern organization, an imprisoned minority of managers must control a manipulated majority.

In no small way, the United States Supreme Court has contributed to this relationship between government and people. By reading their values into an obsolete constitutional document, the Court periodically apportions power. Inspired by the prevailing spirit of egalitarianism and unencumbered by control from the electorate, the Court contributes to the practice of employing institutional power to coerce individuals to accept high-sounding purposes promoted by persons with organizational backing. Its justices are non-elected politicians who periodically rewrite an antiquated document to suit the shifting power configurations in society. An elite of elders defines its powers and from its sanctuary tries to solve complex problems by the issuance of pronunciamenti. With an assist from liberals, they have abolished prayer in the public schools in the name of freedom of religion. In the guise of judicial review, they have legislated in the field of housing, employment, race relations, and education. Their decisions impose on executives the obligation to coerce persons into improving their attitudes. They rewrite old law, pass new law, and repeal old law no longer to their

liking, in the name of an obscure constitutional ideal. They do not have
to persuade the individual about the merit of their edicts. Accordingly,
the Court, through the process of elite decision making, advances the manipulating state.

To a considerable degree, this function issues from judicial stipula-
tion of the rights of those at the margin of the law with little regard for
their victims. Thus, the relationship between criminal and community is developed in terms of the rights of the criminal, and the relationship between moving organized bloc and community in terms of the rights of the
organized bloc. The procedure frustrates populist will; but the Court is
not accountable to such a will and can be contained only by the laborious
process of constitutional amendment.

The courts in general legislate and administer under the guise of interpreting law. Thus, for example, the Court can look at the general terms
of the fourteenth amendment and write rules on abortion. The Court can undertake the solution of social problems for which it lacks professional
preparation, political consensus, and accountability. The federal judiciary has decided how much sports equipment a school district should purchase,
has found against a school district for not advancing a child from kindergarten, has determined that the exclusion of Hustler Magazine was a violation of the students' civil rights, and has adjudicated a case brought by
football fans against a referee for making an unfair decision.

the extent of government power

American government is an octopus. By conservative estimate, the
national government stores seventy billion sheets of paper in four million
four-drawer cabinets. At the bottom of the Big Depression in the 1930's,
the federal budget amounted to about three billion dollars. Four decades
later the budget increased to seventy times that amount. In 1929, all
governments spent about nine percent of the national income. Five decades
later, the figure had risen to twenty-eight percent. One of every five
persons in the labor force, or more than twice the percentage number in
so-called socialist Great Britain, works for government or a public agency
such as a school system. If one adds individuals whose income derives directly from government money--such as armed services personnel, public
pensioners, welfare recipients, and workers on government contracts, the
United States fast approaches the point where half the population derives
its income fron tax receipts.

Government buys, sells, fixes the rules, judges whether the rules are
being violated, mediates, disciplines, encourages and discourages competition. Government establishes the crime rate by legislatiing what is criminal. Government is the self-styled fighter against poverty. But by acquiescing to the power of organized business, government lowers the living

standard of people on fixed incomes. By official and informal grants of
power in the name of the public interest, government fosters inefficiency,
decides the kinds of output people can use as soporifics, and sets up cus-
toms barriers between the states. Government subsidizes those who have
influence and shapes directly and indirectly the amount and component of
the gross national product. By controlling output and transfer of money,
it affects the distribution of income among the population. Government
controls the relationship between unions and management, sets minimum
labor standards, affects the prices of half the goods of the economy of
LME, issues loans and licenses to private industry, and determines who is
to obtain a patent. Through monetary and fiscal policy, it has improvised
a system of guaranteed consumption in return for acceptance of the system.
In discharging these functions, government varies in precision, in the
speed and variety of effect, and in who is favored and who injured. Each
new responsibility is a victory over individualism. Each legislative
triumph brings man a day closer to his demise as a free spirit.

This enormous power is scattered among a network of semi-autonomous
agencies, each seeking to discourage encroachment upon its prerogatives.
Out of necessity, their functions are decentralized. Facing each government bureaucrat are representatives of organized blocs guarding the interests of their clients. His most formidable weapon is the ease with which
he can confound them about where responsibility lies in the government.
The most effective tool used by government to confuse the public is this
diffusion of authority. When a half-dozen persons are responsible for a
decision, no one is responsible for its outcome.

Government has a tradition of low productivity to maintain. It provides a vast training ground for the art of loafing without appearing to.
As a general rule, the typical government employee is less competent
than his counterpart in the private sector. In government he finds a comfortable nest away from the rigors of competitive life, at terms of employment more favorable than his counterpart in the private sector of the
economy enjoys.

Government develops policies laboriously through committee efforts
that progressively water down original ideas. Moreover, once a policy is
implemented, it is difficult to reverse. The committee commitment acquires
a life of its own. Each person in the chain of its management has a stake
in its survival and in its evolution. The momentum continues regardless
of the periodic change in personalities, style, and rhetoric. A mistake
is addressed by allowing its forward movement to ebb and transpire slowly.

Government is at the disposal of those with the money and talent to
control its processes. Carried to an extreme, such a propensity encourages the purchase of legislation from cooperative legislators. The practice of legislators representing employers as clients and the appointment
of businessmen as government officials promote this tendency in the relationships between government and industry. In so doing, government promotes the canard that a successful businessman is a competent economist.

There are many examples of this affinity between government and industry. In one big industrial state, the leaders of its legislature pass laws for employers who happen to be their clients. These leaders are also responsible for the development and application of an ethical practices code for themselves. In the United States Congress, the chairman of a committee considering the control of the oil industry is a representative of the oil interests. The key Congressmen controlling the flow of subsidy money to shipping firms receive campaign contributions from these same firms. In New York, State Supreme Court judges solicit contributions for their campaigns from lawyers who practice before them. In the executive department of the national government, a member of the cabinet finds nothing unethical about his name being used to solicit money in behalf of a United States Senator. The solicitation gives the donor the right of free choice: making a donation and coming to dinner or making a donation and foregoing the meal. In another department of the government, an assistant secretary of agriculture passes information to grain dealers, which provides them with windfall profits, and shortly thereafter becomes an executive of one of the grain firms. In a third, a heavy contributor to the president's campaign fund acquires a bank charter in less than three months. In the State of Pennsylvania, lobbyists write bills for legislators to promote the interests of their clients. In a tax proposal, the chairman of the Pennsylvania Utilities Commission, a former chairman of the state Republican committee, advises a lobbyist on how to write a tax bill that would shift its burden on the consumer.

The mafia mentality of the General Assembly in the State of Pennsylvania permits an elitist group of legislators to use public money for their comfort, enrichment, and perpetuation. Their techniques include padded payrolls, secret slush funds, kickbacks, padded expense accounts, and the use of political office as a springboard for outside remunerative activity. It is estimated that a half million dollars annually goes to salaries for the friends and relatives of legislators, who perform few if any services for their wages. One legislative kingpin spends four thousand dollars in public money annually for his food and libation. Legislators retire on double their salary. They appropriate for themselves forty-five million dollars each year for thirty weeks of labor. Occasionally a corrupt legislator ends up in jail for lack of prudence, but his cronies continue to feed from the public trough. One legislator, for example, maintained eighty-four of his loyal soldiers on the payroll as "ghosts." He had some bad luck and went to jail, but his "ghosts" managed to infiltrate into other payrolls. Accounts are kept secret on the mafia precept of "mind your own business and I won't mind yours." Acceptable expenses of these public servants include a thousand dollars to the Senate librarian for candy, and four thousand dollars to a legislator living fifteen minutes from the capital to cover expenses for driving his car. 1.

---

1. The Philadelphia Inquirer, September 10, 1978.

In the State of New York, the distinction between lobbyist and representative of the people is extinguished entirely. Lobbyists are in effect
staff members of the legislative committees, deciding which bills are to
be presented in the legislature and how they should be voted upon. They
deplore direct contact between the electorate and their kept representatives and prefer controlling the political process exclusively. To assure
steady employment, lobbyists encourage other lobbyists to introduce bills
against the interests of their clients; they can then be in the position
of slaying the dragon. They provide their clients double insurance by
overseeing the administration of the bills they pass.

A myth surrounds the nature of this government. Folklore has it that
the colonies were founded on high-falutin moral principles of freedom,
when actually they were established on the opportunity for private gain;
and that the economy grew out of the assumption of freedom from government intervention, when no historical verification exists for such a belief. The instinct for voluntarism is pure myth. In part, the error
stems from focusing attention on the evolution of federal power rather
than looking at the activities of state and local governments in the
early economic history of the country. It also derives from interpreting
laissez-faire philosophy as hostility to government intervention rather
than a determination by industrial spokesmen of the conditions under
which government should act in their interest. The rule of minimum intervention, or more accurately consignment of privileges to organized
power has created a mercantilist system of complexity. Government is
less a positive initiating force and more the handmaiden of industrial
power. It is LME's public watering trough. Groups create nests in particular branches of government from which they oversee their interests.
Government thus rules by bloc morality.

A principal task of government is to create problems that eventually
require its intercession. Every major crisis of the past two decades
was underwritten by prior public policy. The urban crisis was guaranteed
by policy in housing and agriculture. Polarization in the cities was
guaranteed by policy that ignored the consent of the governed. The death
grip of the motor vehicle on the cities was underwritten by transportation and housing policies. In these pursuits, government blurs the distinction between fact and rhetoric. Its monetary and fiscal policies
are a principal cause of inflation as it beseeches the public to exercise
restraint. Thus, the government gets credit for solving problems by
first creating them. The number and gravity of national problems is a
function of the amount of money government appropriates for their solution.

As a crisis develops, the position of those demanding change, if they
have political influence, is sensed as virtuous and that of their opponents
as evil. The opinions of the baddies are ignored, which in time generates
pressures sufficient to switch public opinion about who represents virtue

and who represents evil. At this point, government throws into the fray the policy of benign neglect. Thus, the thrust of government is not a smooth line but a continuous series of oscillatory movements whose consequence is a long-term rise in governmental powers. Government does not plan such change; it remains inert, fulfilling housekeeping chores and responding to action when matters, because of public policy, become intolerable. Government is a service organization whose dispensed goodies measure differences in the effectiveness of organization to quietly pursue private claims.

There are some three hundred sub-cabinet level positions responsible for the day-by-day operations of the national government. The primary concern of these bureaucrats is the protection and expansion of their respective fiefdoms. They understand the purposes of government in terms of their own self-interest. In maintaining their mafia operations, these officials abhor making decisions that entail risk. The avoidance of risk means not to say yes or no to the request of a petitioner, but to equivocate by such means as asking for more information. To say yes may prove to be a mistake. And to say no may create embarrassing pressures. To ask for more information, however, requires the addition of employees to their fiefdoms in order to manage the piles of incoming data, a result of which, God knows, is a much-earned promotion.

Nevertheless, these qualities are to some degree in the public interest. The timidity, the lack of imagination, the rigidity of bureaucrats have a benign effect. If the bureaucrat is impervious to the will of the executive, the legislature, and the citizenry, if he is unmanageable and free to subvert strong directions from political authority, if he cannot be fired, barring an act of moral turpitude such as copulating in front of the main entrance to his building, he nevertheless slows down the march toward the authoritarian state.

These members of the bureaucracy draw substantially higher pay than their counterparts in the private sector of the economy. 2 . Their rise in the ranks of government can be phenomenal. To give an example, John Morgan (the name is fictitious) quit his seven thousand dollars a year teaching job for a position in the national government. Five years later, at the age of thirty, he succeeded in trebling his income with a job calling for giving advice to job applicants. To perform this role, he is assisted by two clerical employees and a deputy. According to the American Management Association, a similar position in industry would pay a third less. Moreover, Mr. Morgan enjoys four weeks vacation, substantial sick leave which can be accumulated, life-time security, and retirement at fifty-seven percent of his highest pay at age fifty-five. The costs of maintaining such government employees rise more than the rate of inflation. In the year 1973, the government payroll amounted to $38

---

2 Sharon P. Smith. Equal Pay in the Public Sector: Fact or Fantasy, Industrial Relations Section, Princeton University, 1977.

billion. Five years later, with about the same number of employees, the cost increased to $62 billion. The bureaucracy defends this average increase of fifteen percent annually on the basis that it represents an adjustment to make government wages comparable to those of the private sector. 3

For the average two hundred laws passed annually by the United States Congress, the bureaucrats spin off some seven thousand regulations and several hundred thousand interpretations of the regulations. An examination of these regulations reveals the bureaucrat's supreme weapon: obfuscation. Moreover, the officials of regulatory agencies are regulated by the firms they are supposedly regulating. A variety of factors foster this switch in role. First, government officials are hampered by the intervention of Congressmen in the handling of their constituents. Second, the bureaucrats are less resourceful than their adversaries. Third, a considerable amount of their energies is dissipated in defending their decisions rather than in planning and evaluation. Fourth, they not only must be deft with irate Congressmen but also with the possibility that the White House may pull the rug from under them in support of petitioner interests. Lastly, the top public official is often recruited from industry and is reluctant to bite the hand that will feed him upon his return.

the United States Presidency

A United States President is not directly accountable to the public in the discharge of his duties as chief executive. Unlike European democracies, he has no obligation to render periodically a defense of his acts. The mass media could conceivably force him to defend his performance. However, U.S presidents 'use the media to manage the public. Accordingly, the office of the presidency has become an instrument of propaganda. An ever-increasing educated class wants the facts, but the White House prefers to mold perceptions in accordance with its not fully disclosed objectives. The presidential office, with a material assist from television, manipulates the public in order to pursue a quiet exercise of power.

A United States president is not an office holder beholden to a political party in the manner of a British prime minister. He is more an elected monarch going out periodically among his subjects in the hustings to stimulate good feeling by theatrical glad handing. He does not indulge in dialogue with the people, but employs stagecraft and advertising technique to promote not fully disclosed goals. There is no practical way to remove

---

3   The New York Times, page D-1, March 6, 1978.

him from office in the midst of his reign. The electorate must wait until the next election or the expiration of his term of office.

The American press uses the term "audience" when alluding to a meeting of a commoner with the President, as is done in England when referring to appointments with the Queen. But relative to benefits, the cost of American monarchy compares unfavorably with that of the British. The president's wages and expense allowance are more than the privy purse of the Queen. Direct expenses in running the American royal residence are more than those of the British royal household. Presidential security is not comparable because that of the Queen is more ceremonial. In regard to transportation costs, the president's jet planes compare against the Queen's coach and white horses. Moreover, the president requires the direct assistance of some five hundred nobles. Even in the impact on the gross national product, American royalty appears at a disadvantage. The curious around the White House generate a lower accelerator effect on the gross national product than the curious around Buckingham palace. On the whole, the rebellion against King George III appears to have been an extravagance.

In 1970, President Nixon came to Philadelphia for eighty-four minutes. He descended from the skies in a helicopter which squatted on an empty lot cleaned of the usual debris to which Philadelphians are accustomed. The president waved from the doorway of his aircraft in a manner suggesting a papal blessing. He escorted the First Lady along a black carpet unfolded by members of the working class. The motorcade, arranged in accordance with protocol and battle readiness, included an advance car, eighteen police motorcycles, a lead car and mobile communications car. At the Academy of Fine Arts, where the president was scheduled to celebrate America's heritage, members of the First City Troop, wearing nineteenth century uniforms with plumed helmets, wrenched themselves into attention. As the president slowly and deliberately ascended the winding staircase, camera lights playing overhead, the troop presented sabres. A murmur of praise swept through the brilliantly dressed courtiers. Referring to the Academy's director, one gentleman whispered: "I think this fellow Stevens is on the ball." Twenty-eight minutes later, the President ascended back into the skies. Nixon is gone, but the substance of the imperial presidency created by him and his predecessors remains.

A United States president does not administer the government. He is too busy with ritual and pomp, foreign relations, and legislative proposals to the Congress. His executive departments are run by self-perpetuating bureaucracies. After discharging these responsibilities, his remaining energies are substantially consumed in managing a favorable public image.

University professors disposed to immortalize presidents write history for these princes of state. Presidents conserve every scrap of paper that circulates through their office, and their admirers provide the money with which to catalog and preserve them in libraries for posterity. Thus, these princes of state assure their immortality and promote the prestige of their descendants.

These presidents attract a young tribe of staff men unencumbered by moral niceties and eager to provide their services in making the capo look as good as possible. Whether they call themselves Republicans or Democrats is an idle irrelevance. Their party commitment is predicated on which party label provides easier access to positions of influence. These modern Machiavellians are technicians on how to convey an impression calculated to achieve not fully revealed objectives. Their specialty is cleverness. Their impressions are conveyed through staged events that will generate good feeling for their chief. They learn that above all the clarification of problems is to be avoided. Candor may be the undoing of the chief. Their game, moreover, is bound to command many successes because of the considerable resources at their disposal. Occasionally, however, the build-up of duplicity may become a powder keg whose eruption engulphs the Machiavellians themselves.

The superior wisdom claimed for the office of their chief encourages a philosophy of benevolent paternalism. The capo takes care of the people's welfare, whether the people like it or not. In return, he expects gratitude and fealty. If facts are not fully divulged, it is because such revelation hinders the bestowal of good things on the people. Papa knows best. To fulfill this role, papa circulates self-fulfilling prophecies. In this fashion, he can predict the likelihood of an outcome and then proceed to make it come to pass. The populace thereby acquires confidence in his abilities. He can also raise spurious alternatives, such as asking the populace to choose between his policy or the discredited policy of selfish interests. He can be selective in gathering facts and issue information suggesting that only these two alternatives exist. These particular duties can be ably performed for the president by university scholars. The valid criterion guiding these actions is not authenticity but impact.

The president should never make the mistake of spreading his energies thin or appearing to be inconsistent. These errors may be fatal. By trying to do everything, he may accomplish little. He must keep his house in order. If he launches a crusade for a better world, a noble goal for a prince of state, he should do so only if his own society does not appear to be excessively corrupt. If he champions human rights abroad, he should not appear to be selective in the choice of nations. But while the use of power should be clothed in an image of lofty moral purpose, it may often be difficult to do so. For example, while he may be espousing to the world the precept of self-determination, the public record unfortunately may indicate a record of manipulating foreign governments. In such a case, it would be prudent to issue a vague and less embarrassing proclamation, such as being for world peace.

To consolidate his position, a prince of state should work with the attitudes of his people. For example, vigorous American males at times feel the need to prove their virility. Many such masculine types identify this feeling with a show of arms, and some women encourage such an identification. Such a posture places a prince of state in the position of being able to heap ridicule on his adversaries by hinting that they are sissies. Lamentably, the populace at times does not allow a <u>capo</u> to use his office effectively. Elements in the population may create difficulties in reaching the chief's goals. In such instances, he can spread the word that these elements are in pursuit of selfish interests. Moreover, in their naiveté, the people may demand honesty in communications from the palace. Happily, this guilelessness can be discouraged. But it has to be worked at assiduously. The use of guile by government is not a far step from the employment of surveillance. And computers provide many new opportunities for amassing a record on suspicious characters.

government and the economy

A fundamental task of the government is to minimize risk for the managers of LME. This role is discharged by such means as funding research and development, sustaining demand by monetary and fiscal policies, and, directly and indirectly, maintaining the prices of products. As the government provides these subsidies to business and agriculture, it issues <u>pronunciamenti</u> on the wonders of the private enterprise system. And this is as it should be. Through such policies, the government converts the economy into a mercantilist system based on the control of innovation, output, and prices. A small segment of LME, exposed to traditional competitive forces, competes with results that are at times appalling. Its rhetoric notwithstanding, the government plays a principal role in the decline of the private enterprise economy.

Additionally, the government has an impact on the economy by the management of its own house. About a third of its total expenditures goes to military defense. Every day, the Defense Department spends more than the total income of many nations. Ten percent of the labor force receives paychecks chargeable directly or indirectly to defense appropriations. Huge firms produce only for a military market. In effect, these firms are subsidiaries of the state. To allow them to go out of existence is unthinkable.

No other organ of the government can match the defense establishment in its influence over decisions issuing from the executive and the legislature. No other agency can equal its influence on pivotal decisions. Military appropriations rise considerably during wartime but do not at war's end fall back to what they were before. These appropriations have the support of contractors, the military brass, the patriots in and out of Congress, and the workers in labor unions who derive their livelihood from such expenditures. Senators, Congressmen, Governors, and Mayors lead the clamor whenever a proposal is made to reduce appropriations in their constituency. A United States president who takes their posture lightly may find support of his other programs seriously weakened. These enormous sums make a contribution to inflation, but politicians prefer not to talk about this relationship. The electorate reacts favorably to one politician's charge that another politician's critical look at military appropriations is weakening the nation's defense.

The Pentagon housing the defense establishment exemplifies the horrors of mafia-like organization. The place groans with admirals and generals surrounded by consiglieri whose energies focus on catering to the egos of their chiefs and pretending they are carrying out orders. The civilian officials who manage the joint often do not know what their subordinate technicians are doing. They come and go too fast to find out. The military officials are periodically beset with the nagging feeling that they have to make decisions. The technicians, with the wisdom acquired through time, pretend to abide by the choices of their superiors and go their merry way. The charade eventually justifies the necessity for a sweeping reorganization, and the change can be upsetting. Organization charts are pulled down from the wall and new ones go up. New job descriptions are written. The buddy you used to have coffee with has moved to another corridor. The desks are realigned. But the racket of maintaining fiefdoms remains essentially the same.

This operation also spawns rackets for college professors. Many of them derive sustenance and prestige from the allocation of contracts. They learn the art of coming up with the research product desired by the department and are thereby rewarded by their university's managers.

Three quarters of university research is supported by the government. The extent of this support is sufficient to cause shock waves in Academe by a mere leveling off of funds. Stability in appropriations has the effect of jeopardizing the educational programs initially sponsored by government grants. A primary purpose of such research is serving the needs of the institutions that process research and the individuals that control the institutions.

As the alter ego of these organized interests, government officials, like the mafia, prefer a philosophy of quieto vivere. They have a preference for exercising control in a manner that keeps their fiefdom, at the least, stable. Accordingly, they cultivate cozy relations with power blocs, following the rule of thumb of not rocking the boat. This tendency toward accommodation underscores the need for a second set of government regulators to regulate the regulators. In this game within a game, candor is inadvisable. Censorship of communication provides the means to appear in the best light. The gap between reality and the picture drawn by officialdom widens. Numerous means of deception are available: the misleading anecdote, the false dilemma, evasion. The concept of public information by public officials is like the selling of a commercial product. You tell the public all the good things about it and none of the bad.

In discharging these obligations of managing the economy, an uneasy relationship exists between government and the mass media. Each party presents its case on the basis of the right of the public to be served. The contest, however, has more to do with their respective institutional needs. Because of their need to sensationalize, the media make it difficult for government to dispose the public to a particular point of view. On the whole, however, the relationship between the two institutions is cozy. They both pursue a policy of communication-downward to their constituencies. Newspapermen quietly provide information to government, and the government tries to avoid making an issue of its frustrations caused by the media's management of the news. In the Nixon administration, however, the president's petulance surfaced. Its resident intellectual, the Vice President, presented the thesis that the media did not adequately express the posture of the government and hinted that a mafia-like conspiracy was afoot. He stirred a flurry of ideas, including one that the solution to the problem lay in the media employing a quota of persons who could demonstrate they were not too bright. In this game between institutions, the voice of the citizenry amounts to a squeak.

the political process

Political office in the United States is predominantly a preserve of the well-to-do. It costs considerably but pays off well. Laws as well as offices are for sale. Huge sums capture the offices, and huge sums control the decisions that issue from them. While Senate offices in the national legislature are more expensive to buy, Congressional seats cost less to control. Legislation reflects the money and organization working in behalf of the purchase of offices and in their subsequent control.

The two political parties provide the mechanism with which to capture political office. Each contains fluid substructures by which individuals can demonstrate their charism for acquiring votes. Each aspirant promotes his interests to the extent that he can demonstrate an ability to win. Television time and organizational work contribute materially to the expense of capturing an office. Television provides an opportunity to create a favorable image in a relatively short time through sensory appeal. Intensive organization is necessary to capture an organization or to develop an effective rival one. Television substitutes the commercial gimmick for dialogue, replacing the traditional confrontation between politician and constituent. Abetted by television, the politician is becoming a remote person in the lives of Americans. The boob tube assists in obfuscating issues and in weakening party control over politicians. The screen makes a politician well known. If he succeeds in conveying an impression of self-assurance, forthrightness, and trustworthiness, and avoids putting himself against a rival portraying these qualities in greater degree, he is a shoo-in. He must avoid the error of discussing issues in depth; such particularity may be his undoing. He must make the responses that are least offensive to his constituents. Television provides such opportunities. Its portraits are empty of human quality. They are often too unrealistically harsh or favorable.

At times, television makes the political process appear to be a drama of aroused passion. The game, rather than the substance of positions, is the thing. Political adversaries have to make an effort to disguise their actually indistinguishable positions. The scenario does not suggest that away from the camera the expressed differences in views can be easily reconciled. They are in fact more similar than the game makes them appear.

The political process is most responsive to organized vested interests. The representative of an influential organization merits serious attention. The point of view of a mere individual, however, merits a form letter. The courts fortify this tendency by giving corporations rights of political representation at the expense of those of the individual. Corporations can make political contributions directly as well as through their officers and principal stockholders. Politics used to be an art of communication by which the little guy acquired a sense of importance. The process now is geared to negotiation between power blocs. A choice of candidate on the basis of political party lacks rationality. A confirmed Democrat or Republican is either a crank or a racketeer. The only remaining discernible difference is that the Democrats resolve problems badly while the Republicans seek to evade them. The only pleasure of the electorate is the joy of throwing an incumbent out of office. The decline of the two parties is evidenced by the rise in the number of voters who describe themselves as independents and by the number of persons who do not vote at all. The parties do not formulate a line that aspirants to office are expected to articulate. Each party provides only the opportunity to run for office within its structure. In time, the more successful politicians broaden their base sufficiently to ignore the pretense of loyalty to party. The recourse of a citizen to vote against an incumbent is not a measure of control so much as an act of desperation. The political process rests on a faith in money and organization to produce results. Politics is no longer an act of morality through reconciliation of the viewpoints of different individuals through an appeal to the sense of fairness. It is a rule by monied aristocrats.

By their own affirmation, politicians believe deeply; feel strongly; are frank and patriotic. These self-portraits provide few clues to their actual behavior. Politicians do not see issues in terms of a moral code or in terms of an idealistic pursuit of values. To the contrary, most see in issues the opportunity of promoting their interests. They view the political process as an opportunity to use and manipulate public opinion in the furthering of their ambition. An issue is recognized or ignored and sides chosen depending upon what choice promotes their interests. They make policy commitments that capture the loyalty of the constituents needed to win an election; and jettison the same policy commitments, if necessary, to win the next election. Their technology has to do not with solving problems but with managing problems in a way that keeps them in power. They use only the facts that convey a self-serving impression; they listen and judge not on the basis of what is true or false, but on what affects their interest; they concern themselves not with educating the public, but with profiting from its ignorance. Thus, like the economic system of LME, the political process requires deception for its operation. The system generally abhors authentic relationships.

Politicians are for economies in government provided they do not affect their own pet programs. They make infinite promises in a finite world. The more money they spend to solve problems, the graver the problems become. It is a law in public administration that a problem becomes more aggravated as expenditures to solve it rise. This outcome is related to the mafia institutions that rise in consequence of the increase in expenditures. As a corollary, the threat of government oppression declines as the amount of the public purse diminishes.

An elected public official, in effect, is a manager in LME. In discharging this role, he maintains regular contacts with the corporate brethren. He employs mini-max technique to extract the maximum amount of money from taxpayers with a minimum of backlash, and he distributes the money to maximize his political support. He pursues his own interests in managing public money. What is good for his career is good for the country. He manages best the interests of those who control him most effectively. His management thus reflects the disproportions in power among the electorate.

Like the brethren in the mafia, politicians like to take care of their families. Thus, the majority leader of the U. S. House of Representatives receives twenty-five thousand dollars annually out of a fund created by a group of consiglieri from his state of Massachusetts. His wife and daughter are on the payroll, his spouse drawing a tidy twenty-five thousand annually as his administrative assistant. He sees nothing unethical about such a practice. Elsewhere, in the State Department, a post in consumer affairs was created and given to a friend of the U. S. Vice President. Her qualifications for the post turn on her abilities in throwing a good party. This, again, is an expression of pure mafia sentiment.

The capture of a United States Senate seat by a politician from the Commonwealth of Pennsylvania exemplifies the importance of image making in American politics. First, his opponent, a man sixty-seven years of age, made the error of agreeing to television debates with his much younger rival. A professional consultant advised the younger candidate that taking specific positions on issues was less important than conveying the impression of a bold positivism. The prescription was to be decisive. Speak of the elderly senator more in sorrow than in anger. Young Schweiker demonstrated his fertility by parading an ample family on the television screen. His backwoods manner conveyed the impression of a man of religious conviction, compared to his recently divorced and quickly remarried opponent. Schweiker won.

The electorate's short memory provides the politician with the chance to recoup from commitments made to acquire a short term advantage. Daniel

-81-

Patrick Moynihan, a man with the gift of the gab, and former U. S. Representative to the United Nations, is quoted by the Doublespeak Committee of of the National Council of Teachers of English, as saying:

> I would consider it dishonorable to leave this post (United Nations) and run for any office, and I hope it would be understood that if I do, the people, the voters to whom I would present myself in such circumstances, would consider me as having said in advance that I am a man of no personal honor to have done so.

Following such avowal, Mr. Moynihan, as a carpetbagger from Massachusetts ran successfully as the Democratic nominee from New York for the United States Senate.

conclusions

The government gives the kiss of death to creative ideas as it assumes responsibility for managing the talents of the people. The political process is not geared to such human resources development. It is more attuned to accommodating the demands of organized advocacies. A rule of selective intervention has created a mercantilist system with strong tendencies toward corruption. The line between corruption and integrity in LME is obscure. The marriage terms between government and industry change when they reach publicized predatory levels.

With this rise of a mercantilist state has come a change in the political system. The traditional representative democracy is dead. The voting electorate (a continually declining one) still elects political representatives, but the means and purposes in so doing have changed. The mass media manage the election process to serve their needs. The political parties serve as tools for ambitious careerists to acquire political office through management of substantial sums of money. Organized interests have greater access to these careerists than the individual citizen. The legislatures are responsive to organized advocacies whose pressures decimate the intent of legislative proposals and weaken the quality of solutions. At the same time, the ability of a United States president to control the political process declines. In sum, as the national government increasingly undertakes the solution of the nation's difficulties, it manifests an increasing incapacity to do so effectively. When one looks at this government, one recognizes that the modern world is a mafia world.

Chapter 6

University Conspiracies

As in the case of the larger society's major institutions, the university shows an incapability of envisioning and maintaining a personality of its own. A proliferating number of mafia-like organizations batter the university with conflicting demands. The government imposes policies of education and employment, insisting that all men and women in the nation wear the same size pants. Professors move in the many different directions their specialties tend to move them. Students brooding over grades and courses reach for the law to redress their grievances. Ill-prepared for the rigors of the disciplines, students demand degrees that in effect are labor union cards for entrance into a profession. A precarious reliance on volatile sources of financing pushes the university toward alliances with big organizations. The university attempts to appease the groups threatening its stability. In so doing, it acquires the characteristics of these very groups. Under this combination of circumstances, the university provides a good example of the survival technique of leveling down to groups with whom the institution has to deal. Hence the university does serve as an example of the mafia principle.

The university emerged at its beginning in American history as a private corporation endowed with legal rights in which the relationship between trustees and faculty was that of employer and employee. With the passing of time, university administration was taken over by scholars and social reformers, and the university became a center for independent intellectual inquiry and dissent. World War II triggered the beginning of profound changes. University professors were hired by government to develop technologies for use in the conflict. With the war's end, industry as well as government sought the services of professors to an ever-increasing degree.

With bulging briefcases, the professors went out to sell efficiency to the managers of LME. They became brokers for university administrators, who transferred their traditional role of money-gathering to the shoulders of the professors. The professors bringing in grants and contracts were rewarded in money and prestige. Universities were taken over by managers with a corporate outlook, more concerned with keeping faculty and students under control than with sharing a vision of education. A primary motivation of these managers was to enter the elite of LME. This ambition for corporate association fostered the selection of business types who gained positions on boards of trustees and immortality by inscription of their names on university buildings. As this shift occurred, undergraduate students were turned over to young instructors of little experience; the professors, formerly the critics of government and industry, were too busy acting as the hired hands of these institutions. Thus, the university evolved as the servant of LME.

In brief, the university has become an adjunct of the system. As a major component of the knowledge industry, the university mirrors the needs of business and government and acquires characteristics of the system of which it is a part. Moreover, universities, with the exception of a few such as Princeton, do not take the purposes of undergraduate education seriously and treat with levity the problem of how to educate young men and women disgorged from high schools in a barely civilized state. The more representative institutions of higher learning graduate in substantial numbers self-seeking, uncivil, and arrogant nincompoops, young people who are worth little to themselves and to their fellow men. Many reasons exist for this product; universities are not responsible for much of it. But what is significant is that university managements treat such barbarians gingerly. It is virtually impossible to find a university president willing to state on record what is good about these college students and what is bad about them.

In proposing the thesis that the university has joined the mafia circle, we concede at the outset that its toilers, as in institutions generally, cover a wide range of quality. They run the gamut from the ignorant and self-seeking to the brilliant and generous. Indeed the university, more than other organizations in LME, employs a substantial number of persons of insight and empathy. Nevertheless, the modern university evidences ruinous tendencies; it is the purpose of this chapter to discuss these propensities.

the administrators

The overriding responsibility of university trustees is to maintain the institution's financial viability. With the encouragement of their executive officer, many boards of trustees have shifted this responsibility onto the professor by making him a salesman of sponsored research. The professor who brings in money is rewarded; the one who does not is not. The role of the university has accordingly changed profoundly.

The typical trustee at an institution of higher learning is a business executive. Over two-thirds of these executives advocate a screening process for campus speakers. Thirty-eight percent agree that it is reasonable to require loyalty oaths of faculty. Twenty percent disagree that faculty members have the right of free expression. Most of the trustees from business hold to the belief that running a university is like operating a business. A majority take strong exception to the idea that the faculty and students should be given greater decision-making powers. The Chairman of the board of trustees of a university in the City of Philadelphia views shared decision making with alarm. He believes in the principle that in an administered institution, as compared to a political organization, those who govern (the trustees and university president) and those who are governed (the professors and students) should be separate and not commingled. These attitudes, of course, vary with the particular university. There is little reason to believe, however, that with the exception of a small number of institutions of higher learning, these ideas are unrepresentative of those held generally by members of university boards of trustees. [1]

The decisions of college administrators reflect a variety of impulses: a desire to create a favorable impression, an inclination to give power its just due, a lack of courage under pressure. Often, their choices are more the consequence of fear than of reason. In short, their motives often have little to do with the needs of a scholarly community and the product it is supposed to be producing. They mirror the business values of the society. Administrators can be brutal when they think they can get away with it, and they rely on the timidity of professors to do so. In the case of administrators who encourage the involvement of undergraduate students in governing the university, it is prudent to assume that they are doing so for window dressing. Administrators bestow respectability upon the behavior of student barbarians when it is good politics to do so. An educator can be defined as a man of warmth, courage, and integrity. Few university managers would fit such a description.

University presidents use the honorary degree to cultivate men of money. In a story told about such a practice, a college president passed the word he would give one to an affluent alumnus in return for a substantial contribution to the alumni fund. The alumnus sent word back that he would prefer having the degree given to his horse. Perplexed, but undaunted, the president acquiesced. On commencement day, the alumnus led his nag up the stage and accepted in its behalf, stating it was the first time a whole horse instead of part of one had received an honorary degree.

This style of university management precludes honorable decision-making

---

1 .Morton Kauk. "The College Trustee--Past, Present & Future," Vol. 40 Journal of Higher Education, June 1969, pp. 430-442.

unless the faculty maintains constant vigilance. To do so, it would be advisable to be mindful of an old British military slogan: <u>Nil Ab Illegitimatis Carborundum</u>. 2 · Without pressure from the faculty, the administrator subordinates education to maintaining power of office. He may prefer that professors act as court jesters. He may prefer the adoption of ill-conceived educational schemes to the pursuit of educational ideals; imagery to fact. Thus it can happen that a handful of undergraduate blacks acting as self-appointed saviors of their race, can huff and puff and blow the house down. The administrator's exalted position contrasts with that of his European counterpart. There the position is often rotated among the professors and considered a notch above that of the institution's chief janitor. The president's modest standing in European countries discourages dreams of grandeur.

The litigation craze that has struck the larger society has also invaded the university. Students resort to lawsuits over their unhappiness with instruction and grades. The threat of such litigation has generated disclaimers in college catalogs in the hope of discouraging suits claiming misrepresentation. In one such court case, the relief sought was restitution of the costs of tuition and books and legal fees for a course described by the student as worthless. Litigation also stems from professors unhappy with employment terms and from the university's relationships with government and industry. It has reached the point at which a university president rarely makes a major decision without the imprimatur of a law firm. Aside from the costs such litigation generates, the ambiguity and uncertainty of the law generates caution and hypocrisy.

In sum, the myriad conflicting pressures on a university president require him to become a politician. He speaks for the record, and, like a labor organization official, anticipates the political consequences of what he says. It is difficult to generate an intimate and honest flow of communication under such circumstances, unless, say, one becomes his golf pal and catches him in a moment of openness in the locker room.

Prominent university administrators have addressed themselves to this issue of university management. Jacques Barzun asserts that the university has become a public utility. He states that the tendency of professors to sell their talents to government and industry has had the effect of developing highly specialized courses of instruction that have little to do with education. 3 . Clark Kerr, former president of the University of California,

---

2 . Roughly translated: Don't let the bastards grind you down.

3 .Jacques Barzun, <u>The American University: How It Runs Where It Is Going</u>, New York: Harper and Row, 1969.

criticizes those who, like Barzun, decry the commitment to provide service.
As deposed president of an outstanding university, Mr. Kerr commands serious
attention. Writing just before the beginning of the student movement in
the 1960's, Kerr minimizes factors which were to bring about the disruptions
that burst forth shortly thereafter. He hints at the discontents of under-
graduates. In The Uses of The University, Kerr writes:

> Federal research aid to universities has greatly
> assisted the universities themselves. The nation is
> stronger. The leading universities are stronger. The
> university has been embraced and led down the garden
> path by its environmental suitors; it has been so
> attractive and so accommodating; who could resist
> it and why would it, in turn, want to resist? 4 .

Kerr asserts that the university and industry become more alike as the university becomes tied to the world of work. The two worlds, he believes,
are merging physically and psychologically.

In 1974, Harvard University and the Monsanto Company reached an agreement unprecedented in the alliance between industry and university. Under
terms of the agreement, the firm granted $23 million to the university's
medical school in exchange for patent rights to a biological chemical substance known as TAF, reputed to regulate the growth of blood vessels in
the human body. The substance may or may not exist; and may or may not be
related to the development of cancers that require a supply of fresh blood
in order to grow. The parties revealed the existence of the agreement when
a Boston newspaper carried the story in the following year. The Harvard
faculty described the arrangement as a way for the university to sell its
soul. Officials in both the university and the firm have been gun-shy in
explaining the details of the agreement. A tradition exists in science
that scientific investigations must be open and not for profit. The university has been reluctant to talk about either the commitment made to the
firm or the nature of the research.

The objectives of a university and those of industry are often anti-
thetical. The purpose of the one is to serve the broad interests of the
society; that of the other to make money. Monsanto wanted through the
agreement to pursue its goals through patent rights on products and research processes that might issue from the relationship. What the firm
sought was in violation of the university's rules. Harvard changed the
rules. Under the new policy, the university can assign patents to industry. Moreover, in the long run, the new rules put pressure on the scientist

---

4   Clark Kerr. The Uses of the University, New York: Harper & Row, 1963.

to advise the university when his or her research may be leading to a patentable product. 5 .

In placing the university at the disposal of government and industry, the administrators have generated a change in its financial structure. The shift makes the institution sensitive to changes in government and industry policy and to fluctuations in the economy. Periodic recessions underscore how uncertain such financing can be. The cyclical shifts to retrenchment affect students and faculty and tax the ability of the university to maintain its programs.

the professors

There are some half million college and university professors in the United States, many of whom represent the top quality brain power in the economy. Their entrepreneurial activity in generating paid ventures for the university is confined mostly to those teaching business, social and behavioral science, law, engineering, and the hard sciences. This group represents a potential for social innovation; a potential not realized because they are too busy working for LME. Most have an orientation in the interest of the producer and not in the interest of humanity. Few chemical engineers, for instance, have dedicated their lives toward undoing the vast devastation produced directly and indirectly by the work of chemical engineers.

A significant portion of the annual revenue flowing into the university depends on the deft footwork of these toilers for LME. If they were suddenly to revert to the traditional role of the professor, the effect on the university would be disastrous--or a great service--depending on one's point of view. The proverbial Dr. Grant Hustler comes from their ranks. Folklore has it that Professor Hustler first responded to the urgent call of the United States President for a talking animal. His efforts were aborted by the development of a prototype that spoke a seemingly indecipherable Sanskrit dialect. Previously, Hustler had invented a high energy particle accelerator to extend from Palo Alto to Cambridge, touching all major political centers along the way. By applying a political nexus to research and by widening the gap between avowed purpose and actual deeds, the Hustlers, with the approval of university presidents, have made a noteworthy contribution to the corruption of paymaster, researcher, and piece of research.

Professors provide as many systems of thought as the number of promotions available in their institutions. The crop of techniques includes

---

5 . Barbara J. Culliton. News and Comment, Vol. 195, Science 25 February 1977.

simulation technique, multivariate analysis, classical regression analysis, and bayesian decision theory applied to two-tail testing. The fad is harmless if not taken seriously; it fills the need of university technicians to promote their careers. Had a management specialist applied simulation technique at the beginning of the century to the urban transportation problem, he might have concluded that by the end of the century the cities would be inundated with horse manure. Moreover, the specialization continues to narrow. In a recent award, a researcher was honored for his work on the differential pressure to electric current transducer employing a strain sensitive resistive pattern on a substrate having a high modulus of elasticity. Such specialization creates loyal soldiers.

The absentee professor shopping for contracts and the stay-at-home professor are different breeds. The style of the first is not too different from that of managers generally. Absentees view their confreres who do not market their skills as unrealistic. The stay-on-campus types view consultants as violators of academic ideals. Each thus deprecates the attitude of the other. The establishment professor works with the dominant values of the society and annoys his colleagues by doing so. He hires himself out to construct opinions palatable to mafia chiefs in LME. The home bodies may not feel that such opinions are decent. Stay-at-homes judge that they possess the truth but not the influence with which to implement their revelation. Some of the more clever stay-at-homes have lucrative rackets going, including seminars, encounter sessions, and sponsored research. Absentees may have some misgivings about the society, but would rather not talk for the record. The stay-at homes view salary and tenure as guarantees of freedom of expression. The absentees, at higher salaries because administrators judge them to be more productive, look upon university compensation as a minimum to be supplemented by outside dealings. In the larger society beyond the university, absentees acquire a reputation as practical men and non-consultants as eccentrics and subverters of youth. Administrators are not insensitive to the following that absentees acquire in LME.

Radical professors are a sub-species of stay-at-homes. They are generally to be found in the humanities, and, more likely than not, are narcissistic, vulnerable to criticism, unforgiving, and brooding. Their claim to being radical does not refer to a capacity tò get to the root of matters but to their way-out behavior. They fall into three categories: playmates, copouts, and revolutionaries. Playmates are disposed to provide students whatever service they wish. Sociology departments tend to breed playmates in extraordinary numbers. Cop-outs see their mission as one of developing a new life style, principally by the blowing of the senses. Revolutionaries seek to promote political change by exhorting students to stand firm at the firing line. Radical professors of exceptional talent fall into all three sub-categories.

The radical professors tend to see the truth in terms of the prevailing student wind. They pander rather than teach. They shun the rigors of reasoning. They have a simplistic view of the system. Many of them never made a decision whose consequences might prove a disaster. If a revolutionary professor were handed a loaded rifle, he would faint. Reality eludes the radicals because they are caught in the grip of working out their neuroticisms. They use students as props for their own not fully disclosed needs. The playmates would convert the university into a nursery; the cop-outs into a ritual of self-destruction; the revolutionaries into a political club. With the benefit of tenure, they all seek transfiguration.

The absentee is a different breed altogether. Using his university post as a base of operations, the absentee professor is found everywhere in government: in the Department of Defense playing war games; in the White House cloaking power decisions with intellectual respectability; in the State Department providing the rationale for use of force. He is the new generation of college professor, the moonlighter par excellence. He surrenders his integrity for an upper middle class life. His predecessor was a critic of the system, but the new generation is not inclined to bite the hand that feeds it. With the assistance of the absentee professor, government and industry neutralize the university as a source of social innovation. Sensitive students react by abandoning him.

The government shops around for the absentee professor who supports its point of view. Thus, when the President of the United States wanted to give elections in South Vietnam an aura of respectability, he appointed a Cornell University professor in political science as a member of an inspection team. After a four-day tour of the country, programmed by the government, the professor concluded that the election was as fair as those in the United States. In a postscript, he asserted that irregularities were unlikely since the election law forbade them. A professor not on the official tour concluded that fraud had been committed to the extent of some half million votes.

The engineer in Academe is a race apart. With the exception of those employed in a few prestigious institutions, his mission is how to use science to make money for his employer. His over-riding goal in industrial engineering is not how to design more satisfying work for the employee, but how to design processes that produce more profits for the firm. The technology the engineer formulates does not arise from any vision of progress; it involves corporate revenue. He becomes irritated by fancy notions about serving mankind. He envisions blue collar workers as objects to manipulate. The university develops such an automaton congenial to business interests. His predatory quality has been tempered by labor organizations and enlightened personnel departments.

In sum, what ails the university is the ailment of the contemporary world generally: the view of human activity as a potential market with which to maximize income and the use of organization to achieve such a purpose. This view pervades industry, the arts, education, and, in its own particular fashion, the political process as well. In education, one can observe this tendency in activities that border on racketeering. Nova University is a case in point. The school permits students to complete a course after three class meetings. Doctoral students attend classes one weekend each month. The "university" caters to public school administrators and teachers, some of whom are connected with the institution as instructors. The students these administrators sign up to take the courses are often their employees in the school district they both serve. Nova University is tied financially to the New York Institute of Technology, a school with an enrollment of some fourteen thousand and such eminent trustees as Henry A. Kissinger and the late Nelson Rockefeller. The man who heads both institutions, a former electronics manufacturer, views himself as an entrepreneur who perceives and identifies marketing trends and product life cycles. 5.

The university replaces a concern for the advancement of human welfare through technology with a concern for the technology that promotes LME. The industrialization of the university places a pall on research and education. Research is now needed to determine the meaning of the word. The gossamer spinners are considered cranks, if indeed they still exist. The inquiries of the pragmatists reflect a disinclination to raise questions critical of the system because of the danger of drying up the sources of funds. To describe university faculty as a collegiality is often misleading. The faculty rather comprises a disparate group of self-seeking technicians housed in departmental cubicles, easily knocked off one at a time by clever university presidents. The aura of sublime purpose has left the university. It is more like a factory. The difference between the professor technician and his counterpart in industry is that the professor cloaks his trade with a mantle of noble purpose.

The basic purpose of a university faculty is presumably education. But few of its personnel bother with such a taxing pursuit. University managers prefer playing politics; researchers are busy rewriting the same findings; professor entrepreneurs are preoccupied with the pursuit of self-advancement. The university is becoming a bundle of irrelevant purposes. It provides therapy for immature youth in the guise of instruction, develops technicians for the system, compiles scholarly knowledge on minutiae. The professorial role of disciplining minds to think is neglected, and there is no other institution in the society that can adequately perform such a role. The university's timid managers do not employ the influence the university actually has over government and industry. They do not elect to take a course of educational leadership.

---

5. The New York Times, May 14, 1979, p. A14.

The salvation against such timidity may lie, it is sometimes stated, in faculty organization. Such a move, however, might in fact create more problems. A collective bargaining relationship between professors and administrators may redefine the differences between management and labor roles and thereby structure adversary positions, and may raise to faculty leadership the most insecure. Moreover, power cannot be used by professors in the way administrators employ it. The professor must play the role of educator in the hope of setting an example. By so doing, he places himself at a disadvantage. But this he has to do if he wishes to merit the title of educator.

the students

American college students are preponderantly white middle class and moderate in outlook, a conservative orientation obscured by the publicity enjoyed by the activist minority within their ranks. Accordingly, the preponderant number of college students have few quarrels with the university and the business values that dominate it. Their sentiments toward minority activism range from indifference to hostility. The majority abides by the rules and focuses its attention on obtaining the degree needed for entrance into the white-collar class. Its members react to protest only when their routine is disturbed. The quiescent majority represents a backlash potential. The emergence of such backlash depends on the ability of the activist minority to keep the majority neutral.

Two university professors describe militant students as follows:

> Their language can be direct and shocking but
> they do not mean it to be obscene. One is reminded
> of the concrete, pungent, sometimes surrealistic,
> yet hardly ever pornographic terminology of primi-
> tive people. Their music is rhythmic and vital, to
> be danced to, lived with. They distrust abstraction:
> when they occupy the registrar's office they substi-
> tute their living selves for the frozen records and
> filing cabinets. Their instinct for our failings
> is deadly and accurate.

The hard line of the rector of a British rector contrasts with the allegory of the two professors.

> Dear Gentlemen: We note your threat to take
> what you call direct action unless your demands are
> immediately met. We feel that it is only sporting
> to let you know that our governing body includes
> three experts in chemical warfare, two ex-commandos
> skilled with dynamite and torturing prisoners, four
> qualified marksmen in both small arms and rifles,
> two artillerymen, one holder of the Victoria Cross,

and a chaplain. The governing body has authorized
me to tell you that we look forward with confidence
to what you call a confrontation and I may say even
with anticipation.

A considerable number of undergraduate students are masters in
obstructing the intrusion of knowledge into their personalities. This
resistance to learning has no respect for ideological boundaries. There
are professors disposed to provide these non-students with an experience
of pleasure and to replace techniques of language and mathematical symbols with those of light and sound. The professors play games, performing what amounts to a baby-sitting function. The non-student can be
readily spotted. He crushes the meaning out of the English language.
He cannot connect three simple sentences into a logical whole. He does
not engage in dialogue but flashes a series of loosely connected pictures.
If knowledge does not turn him on, he takes the position that it is irrelevant. Professors exalt his opinion, especially those in the humanities,
no matter how asinine. The price to pay for presenting a subject appeal-
ingly to such students is its adulteration. The development of the non-
student begins in the elementary school, where permissiveness creates an
aversion to undergo the difficulty of competent thinking. The nausea
attending difficult thinking carries into college, where by that time it
is difficult to reverse.

Press reports from abroad indicate a possible breakthrough in meeting
the requirements of these students. It seems that a team of scientists
have developed a pill that after a few seconds makes the swallower gush
forth all sorts of erudition. There are, however, two snags. The erudition triggered by the pill surfaces in dead languages such as Latin,
Greek, and Visigoth. The pill also triggers a high that induces destruct-
ive tendencies in the swallower. Scientists are busily developing another
economy pill to convert the erudition into English and to counter the de-
leterious side effects.

The following is a verbatim undergraduate report:

One must look closely at the decitions of the
employer in many cases. The arbitrator is somewhat
bound to the working of the contract, with the employer holding rights that are not within the contract. Only when discrimnitory cases become acts
that are repeated time and again is there basis for
action. The Grievant does not have much chance, if
the employer can provide evidence of hireing or pro-
moteing others within the grievant's own ethic group.

P.S. I enjoyed the course tremendisly, but your
testes are to hard.

The Council on College Composition and Communication in a policy statement suggests that such language has no effect on meaning and that
therefore the instructor should not insist on accuracy lest he inhibit
the student's creativity and individuality.

Student communications are not entirely unrewarding in humor, as
the following would verify:

> Dear Sir: I was a student of yours. My mother told
> me you liked the paper I wrote. Would you write a
> recommendation for me based upon that paper. Please
> forward the recommendation to me in the mail.

> Dear Professor: Is it possible I could hand in my
> paper tomorrow morning? I had to give my last two
> dollars to my brother and could not get to the li-
> brary to finish the research.

> Dear Professor: I would appreciate if you could
> excuse me from class today. You see my waterbed
> sprung a leak in the middle of the night and my
> apartment is a disaster. I must do something
> quick.

The egalitarian spirit of these days has affected the relationship between
student and teacher.

> Dear Professor: Enclosed please find my paper on the
> lecture dealing with environmental engineering. I
> have taken a job in Newport News after being unem-
> ployed for almost nine months. I am very busy try-
> ing to adjust to the new position as well as looking
> for an apartment in the evenings. I am also getting
> married. If you want me to take the final examina-
> tion, please forward a copy. Thank you for your
> trouble.

> Dear Professor: If has come to my attention from a
> source I would consider most reliable that you and
> I have some difficulty. I would sincerely hope
> that such is not the case as I have thoroughly en-
> joyed the class and only regret that we have not
> had more time to discuss at length the many fine
> points you have raised. If we are found to be at

odds, let me take this opportunity to apologize
as I am sure the fault--if such indeed exists--
is mine. I look forward to the last class we
will be sharing.

When students grieve, the administration has to make a choice between
defending the professor or leaving him dangling. The decision is political in character. The following is from an irate student.

Dear Department Chairman: I am calling to your
attention the manner in which Professor---pre-
sented the course material in Human Resource
Development. I feel that he exploited his role
as instructor to propagate his own deprecatory
biases in regard to women, blacks, and poor
people. He also depreciated the students who
questioned even tangentially the implications
of his statements.

Professor----is sophisticated enough to be aware
of the power of linguistic cues. The code words
which provoke stereotypic responses rather than
define issues. He consistently presented as facts
his opinions which were couched in such terms as
forced busing and reverse discrimination.

Professor----stated in almost every class that
the only group of people suffering from discrimination is young white males. He even exhorted
young white males to take political action. He
plummeted to a new low last evening. He ridi-
culed middle class blacks.

Under these circumstances, I question his capacity
as a teacher. I request that the university also
explore the question.

Her follow-up communication:

The content of the course bears scant resemblance
to the catalog description of the course. My request is that the university arrange to have Pro-
fessor----evaluated for discharge. I am aware I
have the option of filing a complaint against the
university with accrediting agencies, with funding
agencies; with civil rights agencies, and with the
courts.

from education to a racket

Education is a continuous process of interaction between instructor and student the purpose of which is the development of the student. The process consists of the collection of information and the artful construction of generalizations. There are many generalizations that are clearly accurate or inaccurate; and professors should so state clearly, even at the risk of generating brooding and rebellion. In the social sciences, the student who resists the acknowledgment of realities, to hold on to his bias, is often persuaded that it is the professor who is biased.

Moreover, education takes place in a context of limited resources including labor, equipment, materials, and administration. Because of spiraling costs, which are likely to double in a decade and a half, education must be economical, purposive, and intended not primarily to please the student but to create new capacities in an efficient manner. When education becomes predominantly designed for pleasure, it is a form of consumption, not investment, and tends to increase the costs of education. In a regimen of investment, the student may feel alienated. Such students should be encouraged to take courses that would move them out of college as quickly as possible.

If the premise of human capital development is accepted, one must decide what fundamental capacities should be developed. The dual goal of education is the development of self and the relation of self to nature and society. As self, man is purposive and esthetic; therefore, instruction should be provided in philosophy and the humanities, including art, history, language, and literature. For an understanding of self in relation to nature and to an increasingly complex society, instruction should be offered in mathematics, language, science, social science, and behavioral science. Moreover, for the achievement of these two goals, one must provide additional courses for the promotion of physical and mental well being. In addition, since information accumulates at an incredible speed, each person must develop not only as a generalist but also as a specialist in an area in which he has interest and capacity. The exceptional student should be trained to contribute to the accumulation of new knowledge. In brief, a fundamental college education consists of a structured curriculum in the liberal arts, a regimen discarded by many universities in reacting to the pressures of the non-student.

Because it is necessary to motivate and develop the individual personality, opportunities should be furnished for the choice of electives to supplement the core program in liberal arts. However, experience does indicate that an exclusive or almost exclusive system of free electives inhibits the economical pursuit of the dual goal of education. A diet of free electives encourages many students to follow the line of least resistance. What they find irrelevant today they may discover to be relevant when it is too late. It is too late for the undergraduate to discover relevance on commencement day. Unless the student is exceptional, disposed to undergo a difficult labor of independent inquiry, a diet of free electives may produce at the end of an undergraduate career a person who is socially irresponsible and without purpose. Because the universities receive public funds, it is their responsibility to develop men and women who contribute to the betterment of society.

There is this too about a humanistic education. Artfulness is a human need and it should be the purpose of education to develop artfulness. Artfulness and artlessness are self-reinforcing. In the one, a person carries out a sustained activity in accordance with a structure the result of which, at points in the process, produces struggle and then joy. The experience of art does not derive solely from the rendering of a tangible and measurable result such as a painting, a piece of music, or a scupture. There is art in a prize fight or there is artlessness. There is intellectual art. Some art is more obvious than other art and more inviting the plaudits of the crowd. The educated person is not one who solely recognizes the art of others but one who has developed his own and who thereby finds reward in himself.

A major characteristic of contemporary society is that such artfulness is squeezed out of the work and leisure of the individual. With the exception of the few, art is becoming a spectator sport. The living experience is separated from the esthetic experience. Modern technology separates the two experiences. College education sounds the deathknell of artful experience as it becomes a loose structure of electives.

Instruction should provide a balance of required and elective courses with the objective of developing an artful person. A regimen of exclusively required courses may frustrate individualism and motivation; but one exclusively of electives assuredly produces an artful person by mere chance. In the pursuit of this objective, students, instructors, and administrators can pose formidable obstacles. A preponderant number of students are in college primarily because of their ability to pay rather than their desire to learn. Many instructors and administrators pander to this kind of student. A deliberately designed strategy rarely exists with which to develop artists. Undergraduate instruction is converted into group therapy and group amusement, and the professor is not a symbol of advanced learning but a playmate. The students are the product of a system that is geared to following the line of least resistance rather than to creating an artful person.

They are also the issue of the public school system. The public schools operate in an atmosphere of permissive egalitarian philosophy.

The dean of a school of education in a respectable university would abolish grades and course requirements. Students would be able to take whatever parts of a course they prefer. Everything is possible and "no" should never be the answer. His philosophy is imparted to future public school administrators responsible for the preparation of children for college. The energies of the public school system seemed to focus on keeping the illiteracy at a minimum.

To fulfill the responsibility of developing as many artists as possible, the university has to perform acts of courage. The institution that utters generalities about teacher excellence but rewards the professor who brings in a contract to defray overhead expense operates hypocritically. Moreover, the university must resist lowering standards in order to provide a degree to all the persons its admissions office succeeds in attracting. If an investigation were made of the masters degree program in business administration, the results would probably border on a scandal. A collusion of mediocrity exists designed to disgorge masters degrees for advancement in employment.

In the interest of maintaining standards, the university should draw a distinction between the preparation of students to assume minor positions in the system and the preparation of exceptional artists. A majority of students enter the bureaucratic class administering the economy in posts that require a particular technical preparation. The university should concentrate on the development of men and women with a vision of what man can be. The community colleges could assume the role of developing technicians. The teachers, physicians, lawyers, and engineers prepared by the university should also be educated persons. The goal is a challenge, particularly in the preparation of engineers. The university must maintain such a perspective while under siege from professors using their posts for personal salvation, from students with little desire to be students, and from the larger society raising obstacles to its performance. To further this orientation, the university should reduce its output of doctoral degrees. The doctoral program should be confined to innovators. To reduce the commercialization of the doctorate, government and industry should assume responsibility for the development of their own technicians or should confine their demands on the university to a technical degree.

To accelerate these shifts, faculty scholars must wrest the initiative from university managers and professor salesmen. As rising income and falling standards usher into the university larger numbers of students raised on instant culture, the university may be reduced intellectually to an empty shell. The proximity of the university to LME corrupts its purpose. If it does not choose to change its course of action, the university may become the nurseryversity.

PART THREE: The Other Players

Chapter 7

Traditional Mafiosi

One can view LME and IME as a system and an unsystem. System, where
the legitimate mafia of public and corporate officials resides, comprises
an officially sanctioned mechanism of organized power. It embraces organizations that are related to each other in differing degree, and also,
separately or jointly, plugged into government. The principal satellite
organizations of the system are industrial corporations and service garage
universities that provide the technologies needed for maintaining the network. With the exception of a scattering of Hessian and Jewish infiltra-
tors, the mafiosi who manage the system at its uppermost levels are Wasps.
The unsystem, wherein the illegitimate mafia resides, is a motley army,
including scattered remnants of the academic community who do not toil
for the system's maintenance, the non-technical low caste of black and
white ethnics, single proprietors, dropouts, young college graduates reluctant to enter the system, inmates in penal, mental, welfare, and educational institutions, and those with the talent to operate rackets in areas
momentarily considered unrespectable by LME.

    Our concern in this chapter is the ethnics in IME. Of course, there
are differences among them. Catholics, for instance, are more pro-Jewish
than Jews are pro-Catholic. Jews and Blacks suffer the most, and therefore, offer the greatest wisdom. Nevertheless, the white ethnics are a
fairly homogenous cultural class in society. These ethnics have a common
characteristic: they are the most abused group in society.

    The city in which these ethnics live is dying. It is becoming an
agglomeration of frightened strangers with little sense of community.
Man could hardly have planned a better way to kill off the city than what
he does to it inadvertently. As a manager in LME, his designs for streets
in the metropolis make the land unfit for human habitation; formerly serving the economical movement of animals, these streets now minister to the
dispatch of noisy motor vehicles that shroud the human spirit. He con-
structs highways at the city's periphery to accommodate the middle class
flight to the suburbs; and when the highway becomes choked with the traffic
of suburbanites moving between abode and place of work, he builds more,

only to accelerate the movement. By allowing motor vehicles free rein, by developing land on the criterion of profit-making for LME, by toler-- ating the flight of resources, and by acquiescing to the brain drain from city to suburb, man upsets the balance of city and country and destroys the quality of both.

Now LME provides the coup de grace; the coercive integration policies of liberals paid for by white ethnics. The middle class in the country proposes and the ethnic, by his obstreperousness, disposes. The comedy runs in three acts: integration, disintegration, and back to segregation and a residue of polarization between Blacks and Whites. Should LME per- sist in seeking assimilation by governnment fiat, the city will become an enclave of the black underclass surrounded by a suburban class paying tribute to Blacks to keep their urban compound quiet.

Government housing policy in the city comprises a cycle that begins as an expression of idealism by liberals and terminates with the subver- sion of the idea by businessmen, local government politicians, and out- and-out crooks. I recall living in a poor Italian neighborhood in which high-rises were dumped without prior knowledge. In jig time, the commun- ity took on the aspect of a crowded shooting gallery. The bedlam never fully subsided during the night. Violence erupted. The Italians began to flee, and the community in a decade became a black slum.

These urban renewal programs are destroying ethnic enclaves. The removal of housing for a new highway accelerates the dilapidation of the housing remaining near its borders. Slum clearance programs become poor clearance programs for the expansion of business, universities, and upper middle class residences. The displaced Blacks who pile up in public hous- ing projects live in the midst of decay, violence, and terror, and pay rentals pushed up by spiraling costs. The concentration of people and the atmosphere of hopelessness boggle the mind. A thousand individuals, in- cluding uncontrollable children, are jammed into space used by several families in the suburbs. Blacks live with tension, pollution, rubble, and rabble. In some cities, the public housing units are abandoned. Their shells remind one of bombed-out areas in the second World War.

Over three decades ago, the national government announced the goal of a decent home for every American. Since then, many billions of dollars have been spent on urban housing for low income groups. But the housing is worse than ever before. The Blacks and Puerto Ricans move into the housing left by white ethnics and convert them into slums. The liberals who promote housing programs avoid addressing relevant questions. Their policies comprise a cycle that begins as an expression of idealism and terminates with its subversion by the managers of LME.

Under the law, white ethnics do not have the right to determine how the land in their community should be used. The system instructs them that this right is not theirs, but that such determination rests with the governmental and judicial system. In the City of Philadelphia, the ethnics of the Whitman Park community protested the use of adjoining land for low income housing. The town houses were to be subsidized in their initial cost and in their subsequent maintenance, and distributed to Blacks whom the establishment deemed worthy of uplifting. The Whites in the neighborhood knew from experience that such housing has a high probability of deteriorating and becoming the basis of spreading blight. They asked for first rights to the housing, but the establishment thought differently and employed the coercive force of law to maintain its position. The mayor championed the interests of the Whitman Park residents but lost. His passing from the political scene does not eliminate the social problem of which Whitman Park is a small microcosm. "Scatter housing" is the name given to this policy of placing low income housing sites into the structured neighborhoods of white ethnics. The public record does not indicate that the members of the establishment urging this type of policy have asked that such housing be built in their own neighborhoods.

The law for ethnics used to be a symbol of the highest moral order. Its inscriptions on the facade of public buildings used to stir the spirit. The law now is a major source of evil doing. The law is an instrument of exploitation and a record of failure to achieve a rule of decency. Of all the professions, the lawyers are ranked high in mafia operations.

Ethnics understand justice in the cities. For most, the system's justice is meted out by traffic courts, lower civil and criminal courts. It is justice dispensed perfunctorily by cynical judges. Justice works on the side of employers, repossessing goods bought by ethnics who have unwisely succumbed to the lure of LME's advertising. Justice abides by the rights of criminals and flouts the sense of decency of the innocent. Justice is an expanding university that takes away the homes of low income families. For white ethnics, justice means being the most underprivileged group in society. Law and order means somebody else's law and somebody else's interpretation. Justice, either as empathy for the judged or as retribution for the victimized, can better be gained by individual action in mafia style.

Life in the changing city is a paradox. As the income of urban ethnics rises, the quality of their life deteriorates. The environment becomes ugly, violent, noisy, and polluted. The environment no longer makes the human spirit soar, but rather places a clamp on the individual's senses. It tells the human being: since I am ugly, I will help you become blind to my ugliness. Men become strangers to each other and to themselves. Relationships polarize. As the national indicator of progress, the gross national product, continues ever to rise, urban dwellers exercise cruelties against each other without remorse. They devise strategies to protect themselves from the gifts of progress bestowed by LME.

Change in the city destroys its sense of community. The city develops
a man who feels no responsibility for social norms. He is callous to the
plight of his fellowman; at times he behaves like a jackal. Science teach-
es that man is an integral part of nature and that his history can be read
in the extent of his harmony with nature. By undermining man's community
with nature, the city defies such teaching. Billions of dollars are poured into the city to sustain its vitality. They do not create a dynamic
organism, but maintain only a holding action. Resuscitation efforts come
and go. The public relations experts point to an expanding university
campus, a cluster of new office buildings, or an upper middle class housing development as evidence of the city's resurgence; they ignore the
physical and spiritual rot around the corner from these showcases.

The traditional superstructure of the city used to comprise a group
of Whites including managers in banking, industry, and commerce, managers
of liberal organizations, labor officials, politicians, and members of the
religious hierarchy. Each segment of the power establishment derived its
influence from the money or votes it could deliver. After a period of
aloofness, university managers entered the managerial coteries as their
interests were threatened by urbanization and by the encroachment of black
communities. Despite its weak position, the university offered respectability to the captains of industry, as well as technical assistance and
flattery in the form of honorary degrees. The captains of industry, labeled civic leaders by the mass media, found that they could promote their
interests by joining and managing the city's superstructure.

Events have undermined the influence of this establishment. They no
longer speak effectively as a single voice. Firms have dispersed throughout the metropolitan area and new firms have appeared not beholden to the
old guard. Moreover, control of the purse strings in the city has shifted as the national government has sought change in the city through manipulation by the use of money. Additionally, labor leaders and churchmen
have lost their ability to control their respective memberships. Last,
the changing racial composition of the city has spawned black spokesmen
who do not identify with the traditional managerial establishment.

With this weakening of the traditional urban superstructure has come
a decline in the influence of liberals who congregate in cities like Philadelphia. Shake most any Gingko tree in the city, and down they come in
profusion. The liberals have lost their ethnic following in the city.
And since they have little or no black following, they are not taken too
seriously by politicians. A major consequence of this change has been the
loss to the city of a prepared leadership supported by a broad political
base.

This decline of intellect wedded to a sympathetic mass has brought
rabble rousing behind the evolution of the city's fortunes. The over-
riding concern of a mayor is not to plan and execute according to a vision

of excellence but to get re-elected through mass marketing techniques. The subordinates beholden to him manage funds from taxation and from transfers by the national government in support of the capo. In industry, no comparable situation exists in which officials of modest talent control such huge sums of money. Under the mayor's tutelage, these officials shift with the swing and sway of urban politics. Neither the capacity nor the mechanism exists to implement creative ideas. Because of the political needs of the mayor, the city's public employees earn the right of more pay for less work. The flunkeys surrounding the mayor make decisions based on what enhances the position of the mafia chief. They draw salaries they cannot possibly command in the competitive market.

Occasionally, the city fathers have to grapple with the internal crises of state. In one instance, the President of the Philadelphia City Council called a press conference to announce that a recalcitrant member was demanding a private toilet in his office because the judges had one. The adamant legislator was mollified only after a visit to the council president's office to prove that even the president did not have such a fringe benefit. The mayor interpreted the toilet crisis as a desire of new councilmen to show their muscle.

The record of city government in Philadelphia is replete with failure to establish a consensus between public officials and the populace. In the negotiations for a bicentennial celebration, an opportunity arose to use the ugly stretch of the Penn Central yards as a major exposition site. This use would have laid the basis for developing an adjoining black community. The opportunity was muffed by spokesmen of the city who have no mass support. They presided over negotiations that produced noise and superficiality. The proposal was abandoned, and the establishment then went out to the northeast fringe of the city. The resulting howl there was equivalent in decibels to the roar triggered by a home run from a player on the Phillies baseball team. The hearing reached its climax when an Irishman suggested that the solution to the problem was to change the bicentennial into a tricentennial. In desperation, the city fathers moved to the southern fringe of the city to an area noted for its ugliness and stench of the oil refineries. Only the rats rummaging through the debris could object to having an exposition there. But by that time the national government had lost interest.

In the management of the Philadelphia school system, what is not gained in quality education is gained in clever executives. An aide of the school superintendent, a man of twenty-eight, wrote a budget memorandum in the following vein: He first suggested that the school budget be made sexy along Madison Avenue lines. It would not even hurt to play a little dirty pool. The smart English major from Harvard, among a group billed as the new look among educators, suggested that the Board take a firm position on staff development. If the adult education budget were attacked, he proposed giving teachers material to use in their classes on who was really

-103-

to blame for cutting the program. The boy wonder slipped from the frying pan into the fire by stating in explanation that the memo was just like hundreds of others circulated every year at the school administration building.

Herein lies the crux of the problem. An unimaginative bureaucracy governs, whose over-riding concern is the maintenance of position. A machine rules over a complex of obsolete institutions administering communities from the remote distance of a city hall whose corridors a self-respecting citizen would be disinclined to enter. In microcosm, the city's ailment mirrors the national ailment: a rule by politicians who either lack the capacity to see the symptoms, or seeing them, refrain from indulging in a dialogue about them. Failing to articulate the felt problems of the people, the superstructure of power has lost the community's confidence. Accordingly, the community's members ignore or scuttle the social innovation LME seeks to impose.

The urban ethnic on whom the costs of this social innovation falls is the descendant of Italians, Irishmen, Poles, Southeastern Europeans. His life unfolds from a history of folk culture, which affords him some psychological satisfaction denied him by the system. A valid portrait of him suggests restlessness, edginess, escape seeking, envy. It indicates a manhood shaken by the decline of traditional values in society.

His profile has the following characteristics: first or second generation American at a higher occupational level than that of his immigrant antecedents; performs a rudimentary skill within the broad spectrum of industrial labor; an ethnic attachment; a non-Protestant Christian, education not beyond high school; sensitive to the low status accorded him by LME; conservative and indisposed to social activism. The skilled craftsman particularly the one in construction, is more secure. His skill and wages affirm his manhood. He has arrived within his culture, and his arrival makes him more conservative than the factory worker. Together with the factory workers, he dislikes pushy Blacks, welfare riders, and intellectuals. Intellectuals call him a racist. But he is a moralist without the guidance afforded by leadership.

He has seen his neighborhood deteriorate physically and socially. The anti-social behavior of urban Blacks outside their neighborhoods falls most heavily upon him. But liberals loathe talking about this, and the ethnic is supposed to be magnanimous. The prices and taxes he pays rise faster than his wages. He pays a greater proportion of his gross income in taxes than the affluent. He is the slob who adheres to the ethic of work in order to pay for the ethic of welfare. He is vexed, troubled, frustrated. A radical change has taken place in his political thinking. Traditionally, he has followed the leadership of liberals. Now he no longer thinks they can be trusted. Politicians are crooks and intellectuals fools. He sees big organization as an instrument to promote the interests of those who

manage them. Out of this disenchantment arises a suspicion of proposals
that increase the role of government.

> The position of the white lower middle class
> American is one of seeing the organized poor, mili-
> tant Blacks, and upper middle class whites effect-
> ively creating new bureaucratic entities and man-
> ipulating them in their interests. They also see
> governmental and business structures acting in di-
> rections that deny major value premises of middle
> Americans. 1 .

The white ethnic's confidence in the survival of his way of life has been
shaken to its very foundations. His beliefs in hard work, sacrifice, family, religion, are under attack by the liberals he now despises. He is
appalled at their esprit critique over what he thinks is fair. He senses
that the so-called educated think he is an inferior, a bigoted dope. The
very language scholars use about him stamps his culture as inferior. He
is the lower class. His aspirations have been betrayed, and even his own
children seem to have been lost. Uncertainty marks his life. He is made
insecure even by his own church, as traditional ritual is abandoned to
support the tastes of narcissistic youth. Because of uncertainty, he
cleaves desperately to his traditions and thereby acquires the label of re-
actionary. What makes it so frustrating is that he does not know how to
state his point of view openly without feeling defensive about it; and nobody tries to help.

> Where once the enshrinement of value consistency,
> adherence to principle, and trust in decisions of those
> in authority represented key elements of life, Middle
> Americans do find schism instead of certitude. Middle
> Americans face adherence to their values as a battle
> against prevailing forces of change. Someone appears
> to have moved the finish line. The standards of what
> is good have changed. These are people who ran the
> extra mile--who really carried out the beliefs others
> only spoke in behalf of. They never shirked their
> duty. They tried hard to conform to values and it is
> precisely this conformity that now results in punish-
> ment for what at one time was seen as a virtue. 2 .

---

1 . Donald I. Warren. "Anomia and Middle Class Americans: Some Observations
on Normative Flexibility,": Industrial Relations Research Association, December 28, 1971, p. 376.

2 . Ibid. p. 378.

His ethnic orientation is a mark of sanity more than bigotry; if he did
not develop his own ethnic base, he would become a cultural freak. The
managers of mass culture either ignore or distort his culture. Within
his own culture, the ethnic acquires a sense of purpose and does not
feel his isolation so bitterly. His enclaves are anchored in feelings
of mutual trust. The managers of LME destroy these enclaves in the
name of progress.

The ethnic wears the hat in patriotic ceremonies; goes to church on
Sunday or at least gets the family there; feels bitter about racial policies; plays the horses, the numbers, and the lottery in a constant search
for a killing; tries to break the social barrier by getting at least one
of his children into college, but is persuaded he is being discriminated
against in favor of Blacks. Change is not progress, but change for the
worse. The least pure of Americans, he is the remaining remnant of puri-
itanism in society.

He has lost the status acquired by his group in the era of the New
Deal. He is fatalistic and cynical; society is one big racket. His job
often gives little satisfaction; its value at times is related to the
opportunities to goof off. The skill remaining in his work is being
weakened, he feels, by governmental pressures to open up jobs for Blacks.
He needs to find status beyond the confines of his job. Few do. His
frustration disposes him to bursts of authoritarianism. He needs to
shove something down the throat of the wise guys in society. The demagogue who promises to do so is his hero. What ails him is that LME has
made him a second class citizen. The neighborhood was the biggest antidote to the abuse he has to take. But that was taken away by the managers of LME in the name of equality of opportunity. The liberals who
influence public policy assign him the role of villain. He is expected
to react with equanimity to accusations of racism and bigotry as his
accusers use his money and jobs to raise the income of Blacks. Thus,
the well-to-do transfer their guilt and the costs of their policies to
the white ethnic. They take from the have-little to give to the have-
not without expense to themselves.

The ethnic works off the boredom of his work, the frustration over
his loss of status, and the inequities of the system through the aggress-
ion afforded by spectator sports; through gaming; through escapist television shows; through drink. More emotional than the liberals, he is
less spiteful and malicious. One should learn to take his Donnybrooks
in stride and incorporate them into the democratic process. To cite an
example, an encounter between ethnics on issues such as civil rights is
bound to trigger emotions, and at a meeting called by the Chairman of
the United States Civil Rights Commission, it did. The Commission, despite its name, promotes the interests of Blacks and ignores the rights
of ethnics. The meeting was held in the Brotherhood in Action building,
and someone threw a chair at one of the brothers. The chairman, a quasi-
Wasp, was appalled and adjourned the hearing abruptly. To have thrown
out the chair hurler bodily would have been a more appropriate remedy--

a flexible interpretation of Robert's rules of order, but suitable under the circumstances. In this fashion, democracy acquires a cultural authenticity.

Some of the crimes recorded by the judicial system against ethnics reflect a cultural bias of the judges. Cracking each other's bodies is traditional cathartic practice. It reduces tensions. The gentle people in LME experiencing shock over this venerable tradition should look inside their own closets. A good portion of the recorded crime of ethnics stems from police interfering with the mores of the working class instead of minding their own business.

While such practices of ethnics are labeled crimes, those of the educated class in the upper reaches of LME are given euphemistic terms such as transgressions and do not enter into statistical tabulations. High caste Wasps and quasi-Wasps have their own brand of crime--embezzlement, falsification of product claims, bribery, securities fraud, and misleading accounting. These practices arise from stealth; most of those of ethnics from passion. The Wasp caste becomes less enmeshed with the judicial system. They are more law abiding because they have the money to hire clever lawyers who can twist the law in their interest. They manage more effectively to stay out of reach. If the system becomes troublesome, they can seek refuge in far away places.

To a considerable degree, the irresponsibility of the ethnic reflects a failure by LME's managers to communicate with him. The failing occurs in politics, in employment, and in community affairs. Despite this abuse, he takes the gaff with little more than taproom complaining. He reads in the press how the same Blacks commit most of the violence and the statements of liberals that the cornerstone of democracy is the protection of individual rights as well as those of the community. It is easy to make such statements when one does not have to confront the victim.

As a group, ethnics provide the bulk of financing for government social programs. But they have no voice in the formulation of these programs. The ethnics pay twice for these programs: once in tax money and again in the destruction of the quality of their life. The mass media ignore them. The Republicans deceive them. The Democrats treat them like lepers. And when these ethnics grumble about these programs, liberals accuse them of bigotry and stupidity. The ethnics represent the swindled majority. They are the convenient fall guys of LME.

Public television is an example of this swindle. Non-commercial television operates as a private preserve of upper-class whites and fawning Blacks who manipulate public money to promote their own tastes and attitudes. A sizable portion of financial support for the medium comes from direct government contributions. The remainder derives from foundations and personal contributions, each of which is sheltered by law. Thus, directly and indirectly, the ethnics are the principal supporters of public

television. The medium uses their money to promote public policy not of
their liking and without the opportunity to refute. The Black Perspective
program on public television provides an example. Its black interviewers
offer points of view that purportedly promote the interests of their race.
The white politicians interviewed by these people do not indicate who is
to pay for serving these interests. It is not good politics to do so.
Moreover, the medium provides no opportunities for effective ethnic
spokesmen to make rebuttals. Ethnics thus support programming that ex-
cludes their point of view. The law providing public funding for such
programs states that programming should not discriminate against particular groups in the community. Public television does discriminate--against
ethnics.

Shifts in language reflect changes in the cultural attitudes of a
society. "Honor," "duty," "courage," are common terms in the language of
ethnics such as Italian-Americans. The words persist to some extent in
the surviving European culture, but have disappeared in the language of
LME. These values generate losses for those who abide by them. There
are no good guys and bad guys on social questions, but ethnics consistently are labeled as bad guys.

Moreover, the educated people of LME have created a technology in which
the blue collar ethnic is indistinguishable from the machine. The advantages and disadvantages of technology are unevenly distributed: the educated people acquire for themselves the advantages in profits and prestige
while the ethnics get the disadvantages in humdrum jobs, disease, and
death. The one prospers as the other becomes an object of experimenta-
tion. The ethnics provide the human fodder with which to extend testing
beyond the laboratory mice. If a technology has a carcinogenic effect,
it does not attack the managers, scientists, and engineers who produce it,
but the ethnics who have to die in ample numbers before society becomes
concerned. These losses reflect the lack of political leverage. If they
were to organize, they might want to steal a chapter from Blacks. They will
find LME receptive if they threaten disruption.

The white ethnic's view of Blacks obstructs an urban consensus. He
converts his perception of the black sub-proletariat into a stereotype
of all Blacks and sees thereby men of loose morals and no ambition. He
is unaware of the distinction made between members of his own ethnic group
by his parents and grandparents. Working class Italians, for example,
looked upon those who had little to do but hang around corners as cafoni.
But the problem of the sub-proletariat is more acute today than it was in
the days of the Italian cafoni.

Sadists do exist in the ranks of ethnics. But they are by far out-
numbered by persons perplexed by the change imposed on them by others.
They are inclined more than the professional people of LME to make sacrifices in behalf of an ideal and in the interest of the whole, There is

more joy, more honesty, more affection in their lives than in those of the higher classes.

The city of these ethnics as a community of trust is dying. Their educational, social, and esthetic standards are threatened by the creature of liberalism: a welfare class hooked on state support. If Blacks cajole other Blacks to act along racist lines, the plea is deemed worthy. If ethnics, in reaction, become race conscious in defense of their standards, their behavior is termed deplorable. Thus, two standards of responsibility emerge: one for Blacks, whose irresponsibility is excusable and one for the ethnics. The parochial schools of the ethnics, a major public civilizing force in the city, (an institution, paradoxically, that has given Blacks an opportunity to escape the public school jungle) is being bludgeoned into extinction in the name of separation of Church and State. Organized society plays a game in which ethnics play the role of losers.

The criticisms leveled by society against the ethnics reflect the values of the critic. For example, liberals in hot pursuit of fame and fortune may judge Italian ethnics as lacking in competitive drive and organization. But Italians may consider the competitive spirit as a form of greed and an indication of madness. Jewishness is a convincing commodity to Jews, but a cult of Italianness would strike Italians as absurd. The persons who try to arouse interest in one may be pushing a not fully disclosed racket. Italians are disinclined to organize either for or against differences. The abuse they take from LME over the mafia reflects their tolerance.

The fortunes and relationships of ethnics have varied over the years. The Jews who first came in large numbers to the United States as immigrants identified with the Christian working classes. They had empathy for and provided leadership for the ethnic. They worked side by side with him or her, as in the clothing industry, and became spokesmen by virtue of their greater education and competence in the English language. They shared each other's culture. With more education and drive for social success, they climbed the socio-economic ladder faster than the Christian ethnics, acquiring influential positions in the film industry, the mass media, banking and finance, and education.

Unhappily, the association withered away. The descendants of Jewish street intellectuals rose into ivory towers and developed the art of romantic introspection, proclaiming from them a wisdom superior to that of the ethnics. They became the unofficial bellyachers of society and the self-appointed custodians of American intellectuality. Their troubled spirit soon dominated the published output of intellectualitv. Lacking an intellectual guidance of his own, the ethnic reacted to social issues in a way that bordered on illness. He lost access to the published record. The society spoke about him, but he was unable to talk back. The relationship between Jew and Christian ethnic changed from affection to mistrust.

The alienation was the nation's loss. Jewish intellectuality lost the base necessary for social movements to succeed. By so doing Jewish intellectuality became a sterile game of ego-tripping.

The loss to the society is incalculable. A wall of silence exists around the stresses felt by ethnics. Americans do not like to talk about them, either because of an unwillingness to face up to these realities or because of a fear of offending sensibilities. These shifting cultural currents have had a profound effect on the ability of LME to solve its problems. It has the knowledge but cannot muster the will. The choices made violate the sense of fairness and polarize the community. As the government deploys an increasing proportion of the economy's resources in the pursuit of justice, the sense of injustice increases. The society lacks intellectual leadership. The Jewish intellectuals indulge in soul searching, and the sparse group of unpublished Catholic intellectuals in bizarre behavior. No reformist coalition is possible, and LME continues on its merry way.

The isolation of the humanistic spirit of Italian Americans is a special loss to social innovation. There is an Italian culture within the society. It does not comprise necessarily a knowledge of Italian language or of Italy. Rather, it constitutes an extraordinary reconciliation of individualism and moral obligation. It alerts us to big organization's propensity for corruption. It provides us with the minimum requisite of an organized society: civility. Together, they are the warp and woof of a viable society.

Italian Americans are not as efficiently organized as Jews and Blacks. Because of Italian history, they are suspicious of group solutions beyond the family and tend to make judgments of individuals rather than of groups. In the City of New York, they are the biggest white ethnic group. The Jews of that city exercise considerable political influence and vote Jewishness. The Italian Americans in a mayoralty election gave more votes to the Jewish candidate than they did to the Italian American candidate. The Jewish candidate exhibited a greater humanistic spirit. When the rewards of victory were distributed, the Italian American vote was ignored. Italian Americans rate low in other indices as well. In an inquiry on ethnic groups in New York of Blacks, Puerto Ricans, Irish, Jews, and Italians, the Italians rated lowest in people hospitalized for mental illness. They also rate low in the maintenance of property values. According to the 1975 edition of McMichaells' Appraising Manual, Italians have depressing effects on real estate values second only after Blacks. 3.

Trade unionism and labor relations have provided many opportunities for ethnics to rise into positions of status and influence. The rise injects new virulence into tired Wasp blood. Not only Italians, but also Irishmen and Blacks, and other forms of low life, gain a chance to become

---

3. The New York Times, December 26, 1976.

decision makers. It is not uncommon for a labor arbitrator to chair a
hearing with a Black reading the riot act to a meek Wasp in behalf of a
white ethnic. It is not uncommon to observe white ethnics testifying
against members of their own ethnic group in protecting the job of a Black.
They act out of a sense of fairness for a particular individual. There
is talent in these ranks, a capacity that injects humanism into the operations of LME. Carl Sandburg, a Scandinavian ethnic, observed in his life-
time that an important history could be written on the contribution of the
sons of immigrant minorities to the redemption of American society.

To a considerable degree, the New Deal's grant of power to the worker
triggered the rise of ethnics into positions of status. The bitterness
with which those of means look back at the New Deal and the nostalgia with
which ethnics view the era of Franklin Delano Roosevelt are not a mark of
simple fantasy. This historical fact escapes the descendants of the ethnic
immigrant. The New Deal was a triumph of decency. The Wagner Act of 1935,
giving blue collar workers the right to organize and bargain collectively,
provided the basis for a reallocation of power. Its critics assert that
the labor law was one-sided. It was. Blue collar workers tamed organization by counter organization. The rules were changed in the interest of
curtailing profit making to introduce more humanism into the process of decision making.

Tony Anastasio, former boss of the Brooklyn Longshoremen, was an ethnic
of that era. Tony was a short, stout man who looked much older than his
years. He spelled his name with an "o" and sued to express his annoyance
with the intelligent people of the press for spelling his name incorrectly.
He was born in a barren region of Calabria in Southern Italy, where the
peasants used to manage through prodigious efforts to grow beans from the
stone of dried-up streams. As nature in Calabria is unresponsive to the
efforts of people, so the people are unresponsive to each other. They
appear, to paraphrase Edwin Markham, as things that grieve not with the
emptiness of ages on their faces. Gentle Wasps readily label them criminal types. Tony was such a person.

A Brooklyn waterfront longshoreman local could be hardly more than a
table and benches in a former retail store. Tony's operation was a little
bigger. His headquarters formerly housed a Swedish saloon forbidden to the
Italians in the neighborhood. The Italians finally busted up the block.
Where the floor show used to be, the longshoremen played briscola. Tony's
office, equipped with an expensive mahogany desk and a red leather chair,
was in the rear of the hall.

Tony came from a family of eight brothers, six of whom migrated to the
United States with their father. They moved into a neighborhood whose

departing Swedes gave them the stigma of inferiority. The neighborhood was a short walk from the port, to which five of the brothers gravitated. One--Albert--was murdered in a barber chair. Another--Salvatore--became a Roman Catholic priest. Tony never went to school, but learned quickly how to succeed under LME rules. He had begun hard labor at the age of eleven, determined to acquire success in the context of the values of the society in which he found himself.

Tony gave the impression of weariness and hostility. Why should he look warm? His life was ugly. But with a little prodding he would become animated. He resented the suggestion of criminality which he felt newspapers fostered, stressing he never had been convicted of a felony. His most bitter feelings were aroused by what he considered the failure of the national union to recognize his role as a waterfront leader. He used to like to point out that some seventy percent of the New York longshoremen were of Italian origin, compared to sixteen percent Irish, and six percent Black. Although the union had given him the title of vice-president, he was rarely consulted or called to meetings of the executive council. He saw no reason therefore, to abide by decisions which he had no part in making.

The Italians of his generation considered the word "Irish" as synonymous with "American". Tony enjoyed taking advantage of the opportunity to twit the noses of this superior race, a feeling shared by the longshoremen. They got a lift in seeing one of their own giving superior Americans a rough time. Tony's status reflected upon his followers. He could be rough to deal with, but he represented a thorn in the side of those commonly disliked. He began his rise to power as a stevedoring contractor. He used the job as a means of gaining the loyalty of his fellow countrymen. By getting his paesani to join different locals, he captured control of one organization after another. The tactic was simple and effective: He would wait until his followers had a majority of the potential vote and then propose consolidation of the local with his organization. Through this strategy, he succeeded in putting together an organization of seven thousand men.

He saw little difference between the job of a labor leader and that of a politician. Both functioned to serve their constituents, not to change their tastes and values. To Tony, the labor leader who suggested such change was a hypocrite, since he would not do it himself and run the risk of being thrown out of office. The labor leader is a servant, said Tony, and not a reformer; he should reflect the personality of the rank and file. Ask Tony about racketeering in the union and he would grant its existence. The boys gave what the longhoremen wanted. It got out of hand in small locals, and the answer was centralization of leadership. "How else can you try to change an organization?" he would ask. He would also indicate that everybody in the society had some sort of racket or other. One of his great achievements, he thought, was ousting Irish Ryan as the president of the national union. Tony would spend fourteen hours a day on the job, including Saturdays and Sundays, because, as he put it, of the necessity to take care of a growing tree.

Tony wanted his place in the sun. He wished to be recognized by the labor movement and by the general public as an outstanding leader, but the liberal press treated him like a bum. He had a particular dislike for The New York Times; its pretensions were especially irritating. He resented the condescension of the superior Americans out to see life at the docks.

Tony's organizational skill is not typical. Italian immigrants produced fewer labor leaders in proportion to their numbers than did other ethnic groups. They were down at the bottom in the community. They were the niggers of their day. Moreover, unlike the labor leaders of Irish ancestry, they had a language barrier to contend with; the English of the Irish was a reasonable facsimile of the genuine commodity. In addition, they were not as aggressive. They arrived later, also, and the system was already in control of other groups. Tony was favored by an Italian milieu. He spoke English badly, with an accent that was a blend of Brooklynese and Calabrese. But his followers spoke that way, too. If some of the longshoremen did not come from the same town in Italy, Tony at least was not Irish. His brother Joe was deft with figures and letter writing and thus provided the tools of administration. The blend of awe, respect, anxiety, and shared sense of status which the men felt for Tony was to his advantage. The many conflicts his family had with the system did not bother the rank and file; that was a private affair. Thus, as sometimes happens, fortuitous circumstances provided Tony with the chance to take control of the Brooklyn waterfront. Tony had the intelligence and courage to grab it.

The second generation of leadership in the outcast ranks of American society has generally made an attempt to achieve respectability on LME's terms. Tony Anastasio was succeeded by his son-in-law, Anthony Scotto, a college educated man who wanted to inject broader social issues into waterfront unionism. Consistent with the system's custom of condemning a man outside the courtroom through guilt by association, abetted by newspapers such as The New York Times, the United States Department of Justice released a publication naming Mr. Scotto as a captain in the mafia. Mr. Scotto was thus put in his place. His effectiveness in public affairs was crippled. Thus, LME brings about the evil it prophesies. The trouble with intellectuals who write about the working man is that they have never been in work clothes.

America's greening does not come from these intellectuals but from change generated by ethnics who successfully challenge the system. They create new forms of life among the people. They are social artists. It is among ethnics that passion, for better or worse, exists. Even looking at the system through humorist eyes is an ethnic art. With few exceptions, the managers and interpreters of LME lack humor. If ethnics could operate training programs teaching these persons how to laugh, many of our problems would vanish.

Ethnics are social heroes. They are heroic, not in terms of elegant phrases or in the sense of a Hemingway hunter, fisherman, or bullfighter; but in their spirit to transfuse an idea into action. Theirs is the heroism described by Ignazio Silone--of men who do not sacrifice purity to organization; who can act or choose inaction to impress a point of view; who can wait; who strip naked the organization man; who resist the pathology gripping LME.

Ethnics now fail because the political process has been taken away from them. At times they succeed because LME is not entirely impregnable. The system is vulnerable to their prodding because of various reasons: the difficulty of a vast system to react monolithically against the threat to its pursuit of managed equality; the reliance on law that can be a two-edged sword; the timidity of LME's managers; the sensitivity to publicity; the chronic necessity of the media to report events sensationally; the vulnerability of LME arising from the need for deception; the tendency of the system to finance dissent. The system is timid and vulnerable to ridicule.

Chapter 8

The Black Mafia

Blacks have created formidable problems for LME. The system's idea of how to accommodate this insurgence is to inflict its costs on white ethnics. The noisy black dialogue of rights without responsibilities has produced a mixed bag: returns for middle class Blacks and hostility for whites. In no small degree, this management of change has contributed to the destruction of the little remaining trust in society. Both the black and white working classes have been duped by LME. They share a loss in cultural values that empties their lives of spirit. They both want a sense of manhood. They have both been used by the liberal as instruments to confirm liberal opinion. They do not fully perceive what the system does to them. The Blacks are an abstraction to the social scientist, a cause for the liberal, a threat to white ethnics, an opportunity for religious exercise to guilt-ridden clergymen, an instrument of acquiring power to politicians. But rarely in this comedy is there a feeling of anguish for particular Blacks.

In this chapter, I dwell on the black working class and underclass, and on the organization Black who purportedly represents their interests. These urban lower classes create the social problems that fall on the backs of whites. The black upper class has more in common with whites of similar income levels. They represent the latest crop of nouveaux riches in the United States. The sense of outrage they feel occasionally is when whites mistakenly identify them with the black urban proletariat. A preoccupation of the upper class seems to be how much distance its members can place between themselves and the underclass. These relationships underscore a mafia verity that the purpose of organization is to serve foremost those who administer the organization.

Fifteen miles from Philadelphia lies the city of Chester. The city ranks among the sickest towns in the nation, despite its formidable array of industrial plants operated by the big corporations of LME.

A fraction of their profits could convert the town into a jewel. The city looks brutal. It has a liquor license for every four hundred residents, mostly in black neighborhoods where alcoholism is rampant. Fifteen percent of the population lives on welfare payments. A majority of the adults are school dropouts. The city has been run for decades by a corrupt political machine of the Republican party. The philosophy of this mafia clique is: do nothing unless forced to.

The highly educated corporate men in the county in which Chester is located automatically reach for the Republican lever in political elections. The big corporations contribute heavily to the town's ugliness and give generously to the party. One firm, with the assistance of a prominent national committeeman of the Republican party persuaded the county court, whose judges the party machine controls, to lower its assessments despite a petition to raise them. Chester is a pool of human and environmental decay created by the policies of LME.

The poverty of Chester is not simply a racial problem. If it were, all the poor would be black and all the Blacks would be poor. Every reason that explains why whites are poor can be used to interpret why Blacks are poor. Compared to groups in the upper reaches of LME, the poor are more pessimistic, more fatalistic; more inclined to be leading a harried existence; more short-term in outlook; more likely to believe that conspiratorial and institutional oppression accounts for their condition. But the poor also differ among themselves, and these differences reflect their ethnic background.

the black protest movement

Like the lines of an ogive curve, a protest movement undergoes a period of slow accentuation, rapid growth, and then decline. In its early stages, an increasing number of persons seek change because of a felt discrepancy between their position and that of the success groups in the society. The failure group believes that their inferior situation arises from external factors perpetuated by the success group rather than from their own characteristics, whereas the success group believes the difference results from the failure of the economically and socially inferior group to emulate the virtues of the successful. The protesters, feeling their situation is due to discrimination, not only seek a reallocation of resources but also a change in the rules. Their inferiority, they are persuaded, is someone else's doing. And this feeling, at a propitious moment, blossoms into a protest movement.

From this confrontation between oppressors and oppressed, leaders emerge from the failure group to make demands on the alleged oppressors and to threaten disruption if these demands are not met. They collect and disseminate self-serving information. Their noise attracts the media. They decide to what extent they can operate with the system without compromising their goals. Concessions forthcoming include jobs, money, interpretation of the rules biased in their favor. Or the reaction may be resistance, hostility, and counter-protest. The initial stages of the protest are consequently difficult. The protesters and the managers whom they confront are from different cultural worlds. The protesters may be more talented (though not necessarily more prepared) than the managers, who may be in their positions by right of birth alone. Concessions trigger counter-protest from groups adversely affected by the concessions. These actions and reactions create stress and such tension persists until the protesting group and the reacting group achieve an accommodation.

The competence of the protest leaders ranges from a capacity to devise and execute strategies all the way to simple rabble-rousing. As in the case of labor movements, protest leaders seek sovereignty and not just a rise out of poverty. Their demands bring returns so long as the costs of concessions by those against whom the demands are made are less than the costs that would obtain for not doing so. Thus, the liberal minded who make the concessions are inclined to do so if the costs of such concessions can be placed on others. Moreover, each protest leader seeks to convey to the rank and file the impression that what he offers is obtainable by no one else. Each asserts through his demands and tactics an ideology that interprets what factors are producing the inequity. Together, the competition and the ideology affect decisions about which individuals and organizations should be pressured, about the nature of their demands, and about the stability of their organizations. The protest leaders also fulfill their own needs. The job of playing revolutionary, the pleasure that power brings, are as much a part of the protest movement as the quest for returns to the rank and file.

The protest leader seeks change by working through existing rules and organizations, by seeking changes in rules and organizations, or by shifting between both as strategy and frustration dictate. These leaders' preferences reflect their ideology, the reactions to their demands, and the speed with which existing institutions produce desired changes. The organization of each leader may range from a highly structured group whose functions are explicit to loosely structured groups whose mission is unclear and whose loose structure falls apart as a crisis occurs. Moreover, a leader's ability to produce reflects a capacity to gain a following, favorably disposed third parties, technical competence in maintaining momentum, money, publicity, and concessions favorable to his membership. Publicity is appraised not in moral terms of honesty, but whether it produces concessions. Thus, the exposure of an outrageous act or deception is not a loss if advantages accrue from it.

A protest movement has five major sets of role players that affect its course: the protest leaders, the managers of the traditional institutions making concessions, sympathetic parties, misbehaving publics who are generally those paying the price for the concessions, and media . . specialists who describe the unfolding events in keeping with their own interests, but who provide the movement with an advantage out of their need for sensationalism. Moreover, movements have a birth, growth, and decline. They emerge on an idealistic base at a time favorable for success. As they acquire momentum, they attract opportunists who serve their own needs and troubled spirits drawn to the excitement of protest. And the leaders of the organizations of protest increasingly acquire the characteristics of <u>mafiosi</u>.

In time, the movement becomes segmented. Hostile reactions emerge from groups not represented at the bargaining table where decisions are made. The attitude of managers making concessions shifts from a disposition to share the view that external factors create the inequities to an insistence of personal responsibility in the conduct of the rank and file. A switch in attitude occurs also in the protest leader, who finds that once he acquires power, ascribing the conduct of his supporters to external factors curtails his ability to control them. Moreover, as the initial momentum wanes, some of the newly emerged organizations become structured in the system. Others vanish. Some become led by racketeers, Older organizations become stronger or weaker, or they perish. Thus, the course of a protest movement comprises a ground swell and then a decline. The pressures and counter-pressures subside, and the system changes in the source of managers, the rules of the game, and the agreements made. The attitudes of managers and protesters become increasingly indistinguishable. And, paradoxically, the initial sense of injustice structures a public policy that creates new injustices.

In the case of Blacks, their inferior status was firmly entrenched as an institution in LME by the time of the nation's founding. Wasp communication kept this fact in obscurity. At the time that the founding fathers were proclaiming freedom and equality, twenty percent of the population was black outside the system of rights prevailing for whites. This dichotomy did not disturb the Wasp mind.

Gradually, Blacks began to protest their legally sanctioned position of inferiority. World War II marks the beginning of the contemporary era of protest, in which the law has effectively been challenged as an instrument of maintaining inferiority and has been employed as a tool of black uplift. The war triggered a massive black migration from the rural South to the industrial cities of the North. Its impetus came from the promise of industrial jobs and from government agricultural policies in the South that favored rich farmers at the expense of poor ones. In consequence of this migration, the black population outside the Southern confederate states rose sharply from four to over ten million. Much of this rise occurred in the Northeast corridor from Boston to Washington, in the industrial cities of the Midwest, and in the Los Angeles and San Francisco areas of California.

Coupled with the higher birth rate of Blacks and the exodus of the white middle class to the suburbs, this population shift produced urban cores with heavy black concentrations, In some cities, the Blacks became a majority. To a considerable degree, therefore, the position of Blacks is one of rural poor forced to leave the land and seek an industrial commitment in cities outside the South. This historical pattern of industrialization must be kept in mind rather than simplistic interpretations based solely on racial discrimination and origins in slavery. For example, the Italians who preceded black entrance into the city by several decades, despite similar low levels of education and status, were favored by a less sophisticated industrial technology. Modern technology began to undermine that base as Blacks came on the urban scene in large numbers. Thus, Blacks confronted by a more sophisticated technology, found themselves at a greater disadvantage upon entrance into the city.

The shifts in the meaning of words suggest the course of the protest movement. For instance, the term "integration" used to mean a process of making whole. Now, the term refers to LME's policy of coercing ethnics to promote the interests of Blacks as these interests are interpreted by liberals. Equality of opportunity, in addition, does not mean what the term used to convey, but rather a guarantee of returns to Blacks. Moreover, liberals search for terms with flattering connotations. Thus, racial hiring quotas are called goals. The conversion of Blacks into wards of the state is called equality. The poor used to be called poor before the beginning of the protest movement. In due course, the poor became the culturally disadvantaged, suggesting that the non-poor were in their state by virtue of superior advantage. Accordingly, the poor make progress by the manner in which they are described in words. In addition, the same behavior commands different labels, depending upon whether it is white or black behavior. To give an example, the black president of a civic association is reported as protesting the construction of a low income housing project near his neighborhood. By so doing, he is promoting his interests whereas a white civic association president under similar circumstances would be labeled a racist. To cite another example of the semantic problem, white liberals heap abuse on themselves through the use of verbiage. They refer to Blacks as oppressed and prisoners of the ghetto and to ethnics as racist; in this way they indulge in self-ablution. Their favorite ploy in discussing social policy is to discredit undesired alternatives with pejorative words. Thus, liberals refer to black community development as ghetto gilding.

Another characteristic of social protest is that those who exert influence on decisions are frequently not those bearing the brunt of them. Government decision-makers·are in the happy position of imposing a course of behavior on the misbehaving public without being required to assume responsibility for bringing such change about. Thus, public officials can order racial integration while leaving to someone else the problem of bringing it off. Liberal newspaper editors are in the happiest position of all: they can pontificate from behind their desks and then go back to their quiet suburban homes.

In fact, the liberal is a major contributor to racial polarization. An incident in Philadelphia is typical: militant protesters persuaded black high school students to demonstrate in front of the school district building during school hours. Many in the crowd were habitual truants. The liberal president of the school board and the superintendent chose to negotiate with them. They thereby violated a fundamental rule of power: never negotiate from a position of weakness. Outside, matters escalated. The Blacks started to stomp on parked automobiles. The police made an arrest. The arrest was resisted. The police used the tools of their trade. The liberals cried police brutality. The school board president was especially annoyed, accusing the police of precipitating the violence by using excessive force on what he called the children. The school superintendent described the preoccupation of whites as an obsession with law and order. While reporting these judgments, the newspaper came out with accounts of whites assaulted by the children, including one victim who lost his vision while he was being stomped after the classical karate maneuver and kick in the groin.

While the plight of Blacks is assumed to be the fault of whites, a solution is conceived of alleviating the condition by forcing ethnics to commingle with Blacks. Thereupon, by a reverse Gresham's law, white goodness, what little there is of it, stamps out black inferiority. In school integration, this transfer of white virtue necessitates massive transportation of children. Assuming that the suburban escape valve does not close, the result of such policy will be massive transhipments of Blacks in hot pursuit of the remaining white child in the city. Should the suburbs be annexed to the city, the tricky suburbanites may still escape entrapment. They may move farther out and become country squires. Accordingly, the protest movement assumes characteristics of comic opera.

A fundamental objective of the protest movement is a rise in the income of Blacks. To a considerable degree, this goal is being sought through public employment and income transfers in cash or in kind. The bulk of the funding for these efforts comes from the pockets of ethnics. Another approach is through developing capacities that command higher wages in the labor market. Such development of capacities means making oneself economically scarce. With such skills, some Blacks command higher income because the market places a premium on blackness. For example, a Black with a college degree in mathematics or psychology may acquire a premium because of the color of his skin.

A primary difficulty in acquiring such scarcity is the lack of basic educational skills. In a modern technological society, a poor background in reading, writing, and arithmetic hounds a person for his entire life.

Moreover, environment as well as education and employment affects capacity. And these factors--education, environment, and employment--interact. Low income Blacks are caught in a vicious circle of poor education, employment that does not raise skills, and an adverse environment. They require power to control resources that affect these factors in a way that increases their overall returns. To do so, they need influence. They must count on government money but cannot expect too much in government ingenuity. Their government's competence lies more in collecting taxes than in their efficient allocation. They require quality performance in an atmosphere of bureaucratic mediocrity. They must be wary of politicians who are more interested in them as a source of power than as human potential. They have to beware of patronizing liberals who delegate to themselves the sublime mission of improving the Negro race. In short, to raise their capacities, they must control their environment. To do so requires the acquisition of influence not as an end but as an instrument of attaining basic goals. An exclusive reliance on political pressures such as anti-discrimination laws creates a fool's paradise.

Anti-discrimination law is a minor component in the arsenal of weapons to raise black human capital. The hard-core unemployed Black lacks marketable skills and motivation to capitalize himself. Often, the margin between the wages he can command in the market and the income society guarantees is narrow enough to weaken the incentive to work. In the City of New York, to cite an example, a welfare family can receive in cash and kind as much as nine thousand dollars annually. Moreover, an unemployed Black may place a higher premium on current income than on prospects of higher income at some future date, depending on how much he sacrifices. In the more simple world of the past, discriminating in employment meant not hiring a person for reasons other than lack of qualifications. Such is no longer the case. Under the prevailing gospel, an employer may subconsciously discriminate against Blacks; his psyche disposes him to discriminate without his knowing it. It has reached a point where an employer can be guilty of discriminating against by virtue of not discriminating for. Federal, state, and local laws have created a horde of bureaucrats to fish out this malady, and they find it in order to justify their existence. They have converted the concept of equal treatment into preferential treatment. The anti-discrimination laws are but another example of the mafia principle.

At times, findings of discrimination border on the romantic. In the City of Philadelphia, the Commission on Human Relations made a study of twenty-three selected firms under a grant from the Equal Employment Opportunity Commission of the national government. Why? Because studies of another selected set of firms showed their minority employees more closely approximating the relative number of minorities in the city's population. The firms in the first set were thereupon requested to sign consent orders to root out unconscious discrimination.

The ruling of the U. S. Supreme Court in 1979 in United Steel Workers of America v. Weber did not merely interpret the constitutional validity of the anti-discrimination provisions of the Civil Rights Act of 1964. The Court actually usurped the prerogative of the Congress to legislate by reading into Section Seven of the Act a public policy that the law intended to prohibit.

The language of the Congressional law is a clear statement of intent. In unequivocal terms, the Act prohibits making choices in employment opportunities that are based on race, color, religion, sex, or national origin. Another portion of Section Seven states that it shall be an unlawful employment practice for any employers, labor organization, or joint labor management committee controlling apprenticeship or other training or retraining programs to admit entrance into such programs on the basis of race. Additionally, Section Seven prohibits racial classifications by an employer in a manner that would deprive anyone of employment opportunities and provides that the Act should not be interpreted to give anyone preferential treatment because of the race of such a person.

Contrary to such explicit language, the Court, in a one hundred and eighty-degree turn, proclaims as law voluntary affirmative action employment programs designating a quota for Blacks. By an exercise in sophistry that probed into the minds of legislators, the decision claims to present what the Congress indeed intended. The decision substitutes a policy of blindness to racial and cultural differences for one of racial parity. The Court did not interpret. It is a rule in contract law that clear language speaks for itself. The Court repealed an act of Congress and imposed another diametrically opposite.

The decision of the Court affirms the right of implementing social objectives by judicial fiat. It feeds the argument of Marxists who state that the law is what those who hold the balance of power, or their official spokesmen, say the law is.

The decision implies that a particular group in society should be granted preferential treatment in promotional opportunities until such time as the positions so acquired reflect its relative number in the population. Additionally, by extension, those groups who have exceeded their quota, such as for example Jews and Chinese in certain occupational categories, should bear the costs of such egalitarianism by a relative decline in the positions they staff.

Whatever their origins and composition, the ruling is likely to encourage affirmative action programs, and by so doing, be a continuing
source of embarrassment to the judiciary. The racist policy legislated
by the Court may create demands by ethnic groups to be allotted their respective quotas. One can foresee such organizations prodding corporations
to institute "voluntary" programs for their own constituents. In the long
run, a quota system exclusively for Blacks would eventually become intolerable. The Court will have to face up to the questions of whether whites
have any statutory civil rights in matters of employment. The problem is
unlikely to go away to save the Court embarrassment. Additionally, the
question might be raised of how to contain the Court's usurpation of legislative power to reach objectives, however socially desirable they may be.

An impartial student of the English langauge surely would conclude
that Section Seven of the Civil Rights Act applies to whites as well as
Blacks. The section describes and proscribes discrimination as reprehen-
sible. It could be argued that in writing such legislation the Congress
was naive. But such a conclusion does not give the Court, through a tor-
tured exercise in Monday-Morning quarterbacking, the authority to rewrite
legislation and thereby to proclaim a governance by quota.

One can defend an employment subsidy for the black underclass. Modern
technology is the enemy of those without an education and occupational
skill. Modern technology hinders the rise of the black underclass from an
inferior caste. In the days of the massive immigration from Italy, a
sturdy shovel and strong back provided the opportunity for moving up in the
world. Now, sophisticated technology poses formidable obstacles in the
commitment of unskilled labor. Such a handicap supports the case for government guarantees of jobs to Blacks with little or no marketable skills.
Affirmative action policy, however, is essentially a tool for improving
the position of the middle class. If the skin of Blacks in white collar
positions were suddenly to turn white, many of them would be fired for lack
of competence. Employment policy for the wards of the state is becoming a
racket to make middle class Blacks upper middle class.

Absurd results issue from limiting affirmative action to designated
minorities. For example, orientals are a designated group. Yet, the
Chinese in the United States are to be found in professional and technical
positions far greater than their relative proportion in the population.
The law also categorizes as disadvantaged a person who has a Spanish surname. This invites speculation over whether a young white with the name
of O'Brian would do better if he changed his name to Gonzalez. One wonders
also if the law would place within the female quota a male who has undergone sex surgery. Affirmative policy totters on the edge of absurdity.

If the notion of under-representation is valid as a principle of law, then Americans of Southern and Eastern European stock are being short changed in education as well as employment. To remove ourselves from the increasing absurdity of the law, we may have to go all the way and place the entire society on a quota system.

In education, two major events mark the years since the beginning of the protest movement: the massive introduction of funds to improve education and the equally formidable decline in scholastic performance. The most dramatic result produced by educational expenditures to improve scholastic performance has been the development of illiterates with high school diplomas.

The public schools operate in an atmosphere of violence, of fadism, of consumptions calculated to amuse students more than to invest in their future. Education used to be a form of investment with long term payoffs. For many students in the public schools, it has become a form of keeping the inmates amused.

A rigid bureaucratic system bogs down in form. Innovations heralded as the next miracle cure come and go. In the City of New York a tutorial program initially proclaimed as the wave of the future is called a mistake after expenditures of hundreds of millions of dollars annually. Teachers give up and describe success in terms of minimizing disruption. An increasing number of them develop a combat neurosis akin to that of soldiers under battlefield conditions. The stress and physical assaults generate symptoms including tension, anxiety, nightmares, and cognitive impairment. Murder, rape, robbery, and assault have become commonplace in the schools. Teachers become demoralized as school administrators, through lack of courage, refuse to support them at the line of battle. The new hero is the student who commits violence and returns to class in triumph.

The disruptive child makes group learning difficult. Usually black, he arouses racial animosities. Where there is no tension and violence, there is absenteeism and apathy. The schools used to be a place to learn. They are no longer safe. Danger stalks the halls and immediate neighborhood. The parents and children who can flee from the public schools do so.

In such a climate, issues are settled not on the facts but on emotions and ideologies. Blacks are sensitive to the suggestion that their children's behavior and accomplishment are associated with their family life. They prefer ascribing the low achievement to school administrators and teachers. Issues are resolved by avoiding realities.. The merit of a position depends on which race urges it or which group is presenting the information. A politics of education thereby emerges. And the work of scholars is tainted by such political coloration.

A scholar of proven reputation, James S. Coleman, has reported that school desegregation policy has provided few academic benefits for Blacks.

-124-

Its biggest accomplishment is the massive use of buses for the transportation of children. By means of selective manipulation of information, his ideological opponents have come up with studies indicating noteworthy gains for Blacks. Mr. Coleman has found that the white flight attending school integration policy is so great that it will wipe out desegregation within a decade. His conclusion has been denounced by liberals. However, his findings have been confirmed by other studies indicating that the greater the desegregation, the greater the white loss is, particularly when the desegregation plan includes the busing of white children to black schools.

Accordingly, these government-sponsored solutions serve greatest the interests of the mafiosi leading the institutions spawned by the intervention. The government and judicial system are committed to an ill-defined policy of egalitarianism. Their staffs have skills that lie more in issuing edicts than in leading strategies of accommodation. Blacks see in the turmoil an opportunity to acquire prestige. School administrators are moved by the desire to convey a favorable impression. And teachers are engrossed in the politics of balancing pressures from students, parents, administrators, and other teachers. The system prefers fantasy over reality. The rapid introduction of Blacks into a white-predominated school fosters a deterioration of standards. In the City of Philadelphia, a high school shifted in two decades from all-white to all-black. Police surveillance became normal routine. Black ideologues sell their wares freely, assisted by parlor revolutionaries on the white teaching staff. The school provides the arena to enact the conflict of the outer community. Its top administrators pander to the revolutionaries and by so doing, break the spirit of teachers who want to teach. In one incident, the black revolutionaries engaging in battle against a white teacher accused him of malpractices including distributing mimeographed outlines and taking attendance.

Public school teachers are hampered by the administrator's love of form. Unless the teacher can scuttle the mania for red tape, she bogs down in a quagmire of clerical chores. She checks absentee lists daily; writes out cut slips; checks book slips which do not seem to produce books; adjusts drop lists and rolls; fills requisition forms; files weekly reports; sends post cards to the homes of absentees; submits special forms for excessive absences; accounts for monies collected; files parent locator cards and student association cards; pursues discipline cases; executes guard duty known under the term study period. And she also is supposed to teach. In some of the schools, she controls movement of students under the watchful eyes of the police. In one high school, thirty-three bell signals in the course of a day's vigilance maintain law and order. Its thousands of students perform the intricate movement demanded by three overlapping shifts. Ending the day without a major incident is a mark of outstanding achievement. Seasoned instructors advise novices to forget teaching and concentrate on maintaining order. An air of continual bedlam prevails. The children ganged up on a pretty music teacher caught in a basement classroom. They showed exceptional achievement in cornering the instructor. In referring to the police records of such incidents, a school administrator made the perceptive observation that there must be an underlying cause.

The central office of the Philadelphia public schools groans under the weight of over a thousand employees. Its Roman Catholic counterpart, with close to the same number of students, has a central office of some twelve persons. In one of the Catholic high schools, after a racial fracas, martial law was declared. The principal announced that so long as the students behaved like criminals, they would be treated as such. The students were subjected to a shakedown. Anyone caught with weapons or graffiti pens would go out the door faster than he could say Jack Robinson. In the public school system, everyone is responsible and consequently no one is responsible. In a public junior high school, a fourteen year old Black blew out the brains of a white teacher. Liberals lamented the conditions in society that would produce such an outrage. One black liberal newspaper columnist wrote that the boy was not so much responsible as was the entire nation.

Within this charged atmosphere, huge amounts of public funds, coming to a considerable degree from the taxpayers who bear the brunt of the social costs of desegregation, go into a variety of programs ranging from pre-kindergarten to college level. They include pre-primary Head Start programs up to special programs that facilitate entrance of Blacks into college together with tutorial education to maintain scholastic performance. Whatever advantages derive from such primary school programs seem to vanish after several years of primary school. One accomplishment is clear: the programs have improved the living standards of the mafiosi who run them.

One such program, busing to achieve school integration, has reached a point where it serves primarily the interests of mafiosi in black organizations. Black children are transported to schools that have become predominantly black because of such integration policy. The transportees include black children from integrated neighborhoods. Their parents protest in vain; the sanctity of the law must be maintained. The law in such circumstances is an ass.

The core of integration policy is coercing whites into a course of behavior deemed to be in the interest of Blacks. Such a policy works if only a handful of whites have to be coerced and if whites cannot escape the integration vise by placing their children in private schools or moving. The policy serves the needs of bureaucrats more than it does black children. The children are not served by the implementation of a judicial abstraction. Implicit in integration policy is the desirability of emulating the white middle class. However, the question can be raised about which characteristics are worthy of emulation. No matter what new stratagem the integrationists concoct to impose their will in absentia, they are outmaneuvered by Whitey. If the liberals succeed in boxing him in, his rising income provides the means of escape. The hot pursuit of Whitey is a waste of scarce resources, but the courts persist. They hold to a position as though inspired by a death wish.

-126-

welfare

Welfare for the poor is a multi-billion dollar industry in the United States, and Blacks partake of it out of proportion to their numbers in the population. The extent of this welfare system has no parallel in other nations of living standards similar to those of the United States. Moreover, it cannot be said that these other countries have no empathy for the poor. The difference has more to do with the way we have institutionalized the problem rather than addressing its root causes. We have given the problem to welfare agencies that are either inflexible or have a vested interest in playing with the poor like a cat with its prey. A welfare case in the City of Memphis, Tennessee, is typical: A welfare mother in that city successfully competed for a job that would allow her to become self-supporting after several years. She discovered, however, that this welfare system would not help her with babysitting funds until she could make it on her own. Her counselor suggested she allow the state to place her children in foster homes, for which funds are provided. The mother refused. She continues to be on welfare. Yet, babysitting would have been vastly less expensive than a foster home and the emotional cost to both the mother and children would have been incalculable.

Welfare is described as a right by a group that organizes welfare recipients. The system such a group fosters is nurtured by the federal program of aid to families with dependent children. A majority of those who are assisted under this program are Blacks. A fast rising proportion of these children comprise out-of-wedlock birth. In the City of New York, two-thirds of the children on welfare are born out of wedlock. This subsidized propagation underwrites future problems of education, housing, and violence, and assures the continuance of the welfare system into future generations. Many of our social ills can be traced to the welfare system and the deterioration of the urban black family. Nevertheless, politicians eschew talking about these facts in fear of losing votes. And liberals like to assert that the public has a distorted view of the welfare picture. The thrust of their view is that the welfare system needs additional appropriations. They like to point out that most of the welfare recipients are mothers and children, and where is the man who would take a position against motherhood? They thereby irritate the white ethnics in the city who pay for the welfare system's maintenance.

LME created the welfare monster by encouraging the poor to enter but not providing incentives and strategies for them to leave. The system finds institutionalizing the maintenance of the poor easier than reducing the root causes of poverty. The welfare bureaucracy has needs of its own in seeing that solutions preserve their interests. The black leaders, so-called, cannot easily empathize with the position of the black underclass. We should expect, accordingly, the permanent maintenance of an army of Blacks who do not fit into LME on its terms.

concluding observations

Blacks have made noteworthy economic, educational, and political gains in the past several decades. A rising number of them are to be found in the professions, in the legislatures, and in the mayoralty offices of the nation. To a considerable degree, the persons who have experienced this mobility represent a relatively small strain of the black population. The so-called black leaders have risen out of this strain. Their needs, values, and priorities are quite different from those of the black rank and file population. They are mostly of different ethnic origin, either of West Indian or pre-Civil War freeman descent. Their alleged leadership tends to become a racket acquiesced to by whites in the power structure who find dealing with such Blacks more comfortable.

At the nation's founding, the Negro was a one-fifth person as defined by the constitution. The leadership elite, black and white, is now trying through public policy to make him disappear into the white mass. A presumption exists that once Blacks acquire white middle class standards, racial antagonisms will decline. Moreover, the special treatment provided Blacks in housing, education, and employment will no longer be necessary, and will, accordingly, be withdrawn at some future date.

These assumptions are unwarranted. Institutions have a way of surviving after their original intent wanes, because the persons who take them over derive income, prestige, and power from their continued existence. Moreover, these so-called leaders use the threat of disruption to make gains, without attempting to accommodate the interests of the whites who have to pay the costs out of their hides. To their way of thinking, it is all right to encourage Blacks to act in unison but improper for whites to react as whites. They claim rights without presenting the evidence to support them and without thought about their responsibilities. The limit of resources is alien to their thinking. They win battles at .the expense of the society's viability, and, often, at the expense of the rank and file Blacks whose interests they claim to champion. Anger corrupts their judgment. Irrationally, they seek to change values by a system of coercion. They espouse policies without reference to standards of reason and fairness. Their acts serve to maintain ruptured communication lines between the races. The good will that somehow manages to survive is fostered to a considerable degree by persons who do not place institutional blinders on themselves.

These black "leaders", unlike trade union officials, do not really speak in behalf of the rank and file. They come from different social origins. The opinion of these self-styled spokesmen is unrepresentative of those they purportedly lead. A substantial majority of the led oppose busing and affirmative action and would go down harder on criminals.

The "leaders" identify more with white elite liberals from whom they derive financial and moral support. Their leadership derives not from the more difficult responsibility of leading Blacks but from extracting concessions from whites. Their tactics and public announcements mirror this orientation. Neither race nor slavery accounts for the wretched position of the black underclass. The unemployment, inferior and antisocial scholastic performance, the violence, lack of family life, the teenage pregnancy of the black underclass has to be examined not as a problem of race and slavery but as one of inept and uncourageous leadership promoting policies that raise its status but that aggravate the condition of the black underclass.

These leaders comprise the black mafia. They organize to promote their interests at the expense of those they allegedly serve. Their posture destroys the empathy whites may have for the plight of low income Blacks. The position of these leaders weakens the society's bonds. White elites pamper them. The black protest movement acquired momentum from the guilt feelings of whites in influential posts. The ethnics who are now asked to make concessions are disinclined to do so. Hitting them over the head does not make them more responsive.

And this gets us to another major source of social friction: the violence of the black underclass. The Blacks have taken over the Italian crime rate. The Italians of the first big surge of immigration to the United States provided a substantial amount of the violence of that period. The Blacks today have assumed this major contribution to violence. Both groups in their day were the poorest people in the city. Both groups at different periods of urban history lacked the means to success available to more favored groups in the society.

But that is where the similarity ends. The Italians practiced violence for a calculated purpose of amassing and controlling wealth on a big scale because other options were closed. Their violence had a moralistic base—to redress violations of a code of honor. Moreover, it grew out of a conflict between persons who knew each other. The violence was confined to criminal elements. Accordingly, the neighborhood where the _mafiosi_ lived was relatively safe to those outside the group.

Black violence is more wanton and more sadistic. It is stranger to stranger. It has no calculated purpose. It is a sadistic exercise in enjoyment, as when a thief shoots his victim in a final act of pleasure. It is terror for its own sake. Moreover, the boom of the criminal justice system of the past came down hard on the Italians—on the guilty as well as on the innocent. The criminal justice system today is based more on the rights of criminals than on those of their victims.

These pressures from the dual black society make a noteworthy contribution to the destruction of the bond holding together the larger society.

Chapter 9

Cosa Nostra Intellectuals

Whether he wants to be or not, the liberal in the United States is a principal in moving society toward an equality of mediocrity under the aegis of the state. He spurs such a movement by promoting causes that require government intervention. The liberal is the self-appointed master planner of society. He is the intellectual who guards its zeitgeist. In trying to fulfill this role, he is a major contributor to the development of a collective personality. He is the person who easily seduces himself into believing that his ideas , if placed into effect, would produce a better world. The biggest tyrannies in the course of history have been perpetrated by such intellectuals persuading a political authority to implement their ideas.

The contemporary state-managed promotion of equality has its historical roots in liberalism. The ancestry of this liberalism derives from the utilitarianism and scientism of British philosophers whose ideas appeared about two centuries ago. Scientism introduced the notion that through rational analysis a society could bring about the happiness and well-being of the individual. Science would produce a morality, moreover, based on reason. The same hopes produced utilitarianism, which became the ethical foundation of public policy. This ethic fostered the idea that it is all right to take away without consent the product of one person and to give it to someone else so long as the resulting redistribution raised the overall amount of satisfaction in society. The end--an overall rise in satisfaction--justified the means: confiscation. In addition, this redistribution would be justifiable despite the inefficiency that might result. If, for instance, a redistribution of income from the affluent to the poor resulted in a ninety percent loss of production reaching the poor, the transfer would be reasonable if an overall rise in satisfaction occurred.

These twin pillars of liberalism--scientism and utilitarianism--have produced a system of choice in which those who hold the balance of power decide what constitutes the social good and those who lack political influence sustain its costs. What is fair is what those who succeed in manipulating the state deem to be fair.

This liberalism has brought with it a polarization of groups in society and corruption of ideals, evasion of individual responsibility, mistrust of government. Moreover, the social benefits of liberal philosophy have been modest. After public expenditures of countless billions of dollars, we are no better off in housing, public education, capacities, or in general welfare, and we have the same relative number of poor. But the failures of liberal formulas merely increase the appetite of the state for a more extensive management of human life.

A far-reaching implication of liberalism can be found in its notions of equality. In the name of increasing equality, liberal thought has promoted the idea of opportunity for education and employment without regard to race, sex, religion, and national origin. The idea had convincing moral grounds. Who, for example, what depraved individual, would deny to a child the chance to maximize his or her potential? But the newly installed bureaucracy and the courts converted the idea of equality of opportunity into guaranteed results for designated groups. Accordingly, the legacy of liberalism is a society whose zeal for equality creates an impatience with distinction. But if all of us are equal, how do we praise and reward those who make more than equal contributions to the society? Why should the more productive maintain ever-rising living standards for the less productive? We are all equal in the right to civil treatment. But are we equal in competence in particular areas of specialization and in the degree to which we promote the well-being of the society's members?

At times, the term "intellectual" is loosely used and undeservedly bestowed. For instance, most sociologists would probably like to be called intellectuals; yet the piles of information they accumulate on human activity suggest that more than a few of them are failed journalists possessing less objectivity and writing skill. Intellectuals are persons with high convictions of their mental powers and their ability to provide enlightenment; to ethnics, however, they are jerks. We present them within this frame of disaffection.

. In our discussion of this social class, a problem of classification arises. The classification encompasses a range of persons--from writers critical of society to those included in this category by virtue of a mere undergraduate college degree, from persons who enjoy incorporating obscenities into their speech and writing to well-groomed citizens of restrained language who move in LME's conservative circles. This problem of classification is compounded by the exclusionist views intellectuals have of themselves. To avoid contamination with lesser intellectuals, they assume such titles as "conservative liberals", "democratic socialists", "passive anarchists", "theoretical radicals", or just "leftists". The problem is one of difficulty in finding other intellectuals of comparable erudition. Nevertheless, a common bond exists among them: bitching and preferring a complex explanation of events over a simple one.

Take the Manhattan Jewish school of intellectuals. They have a reputation for talking mostly to each other and occasionally to God. They live piled high on one another immersed in the stench of their wastes. In 1756, the population of their island numbered ten thousand whites and two thousand Blacks. Recorded history states that there was no town where the air was better or where there is a more general appearance of ease. Two centuries later, the population of this intellectuals' oasis numbers a million and a half. And the air is most foul. As their eyes scan a vista of trash, they conjure up highfalutin words and disgorge them on bond paper in the hope of marketing their sufferings in literary works. Many a battle they have won on their typewriters. They consider themselves cosmopolitan, but their life experience is confined mostly to an area bounded on the east by Long Island and on the west by the Hudson River. Their global generalizations issue from mid-Manhattan neuroticisms.

The New York Review is a major source of erudite information for Manhattan intellectuals. The Review pimps for a particular audience in the same way popular magazines do for theirs, with the advantage of ascribing a superior social purpose to its pandering. Its writers subscribe to the good guys and the bad guys theory of events, the one comprising mostly Jewish intellectuals together with a few redeemed Wasps and the other, the establishment. Less heady than the Review, The New York Times is also an indispensable part of their vade mecum. The Sunday issue of the Times on the door mat in front of the apartment door is a symbol of intellectuality inside.

Many such subspecies of intellectual prevail. Today's list is obsolete tomorrow as groups divide and sub-divide. One can mention intellectuals such as Eric Hoffer, the anti-intellectual intellectual who has gained notoriety as the poor man's intellectual; intellectuals whose causes amount to slumming; lackey intellectuals (a term invented by the brethren) who sell their brains to the highest bidder in LME and who calm their torment with drink, sex, and psychiatry; scholarly intellectuals who cannot let well enough alone--like, for example, the one at Brandeis University who says the Jews discovered America before the first Italian to come to the United States: Cristoforo Colombo; intellectuals who play war games under government contracts, who devastate entire nations like children knocking over a line of toy soldiers but who have not been within earshot of a bullet bent on destruction. Some have awesome titles. In a book on China, three parlor warriors are listed as Deputy Assistant Secretary of Defense for Policy Planning and Arms Control, Specialist in Weapons Systems Choice, and Director of Guerrilla Warfare. Big deal.

These intellectuals venerate the life of cerebral abstractions. The malaise resulting from this attitude catapults them in hot pursuit of psychocures and worthy causes. Their visceral deficiencies dispose them to embrace sweeping criticisms of society. By so doing, they forfeit the use of intelligence. The fashionable condemnation among intellectuals is the view that individuals are servants of the system. This observation brings the cross of determinism to its logical end result: the individual is the product of forces beyond his control. But at this point a paradox emerges. Somehow a consciousness unfolds that is independent and critical of the system that makes persons behave in a manner inconsistent with the system's demands on him. Thus, there emerges the philosophy that although the system is not the consequence of individual choices, eventually individual choice will cause the system's collapse.

Some intellectuals are real tough. Walt W. Rostow of IndoChina war fame falls into such a category. Far be it from this brand of intellectual to brood over the fact that the rationale he sells to a prince of power in LME does not place _his_ life on the line. They are realists despite their intellectual standing. Their decision making cannot be cluttered with questions of moral sensitivity. While the contribution of these gentlemen to the collapse of the nation's prestige is by no means minor, they nevertheless garner many laurels and pass on to positions of eminence in LME. Princes of power shield them from the working class, whose suspicion of such a type of intellectual manifests political acumen.

Within the broad array of intellectuals is a small band that comprises the new left. Their revolutionary role is prudently confined to giving support to protesting youth. Theirs is a quixotic kind of logic. The violence committed by the system, they assert, is similar to that of Nazi Germany. Therefore, to commit acts of violence against the system is a worthy moral act. Analogously, the propriety of an act of violence depends upon the sympathy one has for the person who exercises it. Once you decide an official is a baddy, it is all right to label him a criminal without due process. Once so labeled, committing violence against him is a superior moral act.

Of all the intellectual varieties, the Roman Catholic leftist is the most bizarre. He and his disciples possess an awe for pure moral posture and a disdain for political strategy; if one asks them for specifics on their assertions, they begin to brood. Comprised mainly of elements of British and Irish origin, they are the eternal wonder of the Italian contingent of the Church. They have discovered sin in society and the discovery is a heavy burden. In observing their enactment of a morality play, one must restrain the urge to applaud. Come the revolution, they will provide a backdrop of poetry and lyre.

Scratch a Catholic leftist and one finds a man who believes his thought is of a high moral order. Convinced of his righteousness, he arrogates to himself the task of determining who in society promotes goodness and who badness. Goodies earn approbation, and baddies condemnation. He decides whose conduct is worthy and hence entitled to exemption from the rules. He starts from lofty universal principles and then bestows rights of exception on the chosen. He begins with the principle of non-violence and proceeds to corrupt it; he starts with individual moral responsibility and corrupts that too. His contribution to the new logic runs as follows: If a cause is just, then all actions performed to further the cause are non-violent. A cause is just if its adherents believe it is. Conclusion: critics of their causes are immoral. Accordingly, they have rediscovered Kant's categorical imperative.

They have not been spared by the conspiracy syndrome prevailing in society. The conspirators are the national government and the managers in LME. The Catholic left sees conspiracy in foreign and domestic oppression. Non-Catholic adherents to the conspiracy theory make the idea more lusty. Discussing technology, for instance, Theodore Roszak states:

> Such statements (of a former Secretary of Defense) uttered by obviously competent, obviously enlightened leadership, make abundantly clear the prime strategy of the technocracy. It is to level life down to a standard of so-called living that technical expertise can cope with and then, on that false and exclusive basis, to claim an intimidating omnicompetence over us by its monopoly of the experts.

> To liberate sexuality would be to create a society in which technocratic discipline would be impossible. But to thwart sexuality outright would create a widespread, explosive resentment that requires constant policing; and besides, this would associate the technocracy with various puritanical traditions that enlightened men cannot but regard as superstitious. The strategy chosen, therefore, is not harsh repression, but rather the Playboy version of total permissiveness. In the affluent society, we have sex and sex galore--or so we are to believe. But when we look more closely we see that this sybaritic promiscuity wears a special social coloring. It has been assimilated to an income level and social status available only to our well-heeled junior executives and the jet set. 1.

It is my observation that the young students Roszak champions acquire more sex galore than do the junior executives--at less expense.

---

1. Theodore Roszak. The Making of a Counter Culture, New York: Doubleday, 1969.

Of the militant Catholic left, Ned O'Gorman writes:

> In the militant Catholic left--and in the Black
> militant left, too--there is an irrationality that
> taints the revolution and limits its chances of
> success. I write of that crippled, howling, petulant
> spoiled brat anger, and the self-importance that entraps
> revolutionaries in their own will and leaves their zeal,
> their visions and their hope abandoned to their egos
> and to the collective egos of their followers. I am
> not sure if I can bear any more the small voice crying
> alone in the wilderness. One seeks the solitary sear-
> ing voice of the prophet but I want to hear it in the
> street, in the world, in schools, in politics where
> change is still possible. The Catholic left has nur-
> tured a community of parasites who free-load off the
> Gospels. 2 .

Most of these intellectuals are liberals. Few of them would quarrel
with such an assertion. But not all liberals are intellectuals. For example,
a man not disposed to shock when hearing an obscenity is liberal minded, but
not necessarily intellectual. But if he uses four-letter words in his own
speech and writing, he merits the title of intellectual. The confusion raised
by these fine distinctions diminish as liberals, out of frustration, become
intellectuals. For a liberal in these times is weighted down with pessimistic
thoughts. He bears the burden of fighting oppression, racism, and antisemites.
He is the American version of Ibsen's Brand.

Liberals make a heavy contribution to the social ills they deplore.
Those who fight for community integration are principals in its destruction.
Within their ranks are persons who are racist, intolerant, and ill-informed.
Driven up the wall, they accuse their critics of lack of compassion and in-
tellectual strength, qualities which they claim in abundance for themselves.
They are without humor.

Liberals often make their startling revelations in the press. Down at
the bottom of the editorial information, under a formidable list of under-
writers of the new faith, non-luminaries can indicate their spiritual and
financial allegiance by marking the appropriate square and sending a check.
No space is provided for rebuttal. The principals who write such statements
are persons the academic profession refers to as scholars.

---

2. The New York Times, May 30, 1971.

At times, the distinction between liberalism and conservatism is one of disposition arising from dissimilarity in body chemistry. Body enzymes trigger differences in perceiving the same phenomena. Thus, in observing a noisy group of Blacks a liberal uses the term boisterous for what a conservative would describe as a howling mob; in referring to a teenage rioter, the one would say impressionable youngster; the other, hoodlum. They choose sides: Thus, the liberal may state we have to relate, and the conservative, call the cops. Moreover, the same verbiage can convey different meanings. To a conservative chemistry professor, the term "heavily doped semi-conductor" connotes a chemical reaction. To a liberal humanities professor, it may conjure up a hippy.

Many of the propositions lofted by intellectuals are unassailable; while their terms lack precision, they nevertheless convey good intent. For example, when it is asserted that the mission of the individual is recovery of self, who would criticise such a worthy restoration? But they do not let well enough alone; they indulge in exposition. By so doing, when they cite that the recovery involves freedom from parents, school, career, and the English language, they take a massive step toward the brink of absurdity. And when they go on to suggest that such youth will lead the working class toward the same redemption, they plunge in head first.

Despite its lack of precision, the term "liberal" is useful as a generic description of persons disposed to see things change. As a general classification, it serves the purpose of lumping together the dissenters: from pragmatists who are receptive to new courses of action, generally at someone else's expense, to neurotics whose perturbations incline them to be abrasive.

Therefore, we launch the hypothesis that intellectuals are mostly liberal, but liberals cannot automatically claim the title of intellectual; nor would many of them want to. One must keep in mind as well the many categories of the subspecies. Thus, in a university, the general class "college professor" can be divided into a variety of subclasses. There are the dutiful who prepare their lessons conscientiously and take their cues from administrators. There are dissenters who stir things up at meetings, who rarely hazard proposals of their own, but stand every ready to pounce on the ideas of others. To use the terms of Harvard professor Crane Brinton, this group can be classified as bellyachers. The most profound liberals, certainly, are professors who talk and write extensively on social movements without ever referring to any one social problem in particular. Their ability to produce abstract words is inversely proportional to their capacity to construct a social movement. Their strategy includes the invention of new terms for old phenomena and the use of charged words to control thought. For example, a liberal would term "genocide" society's restrictions on a woman copulating at public expense. And he would refer to a black neighborhood as a "ghetto."

In a clash of opinion among themselves, liberals often behave like children, accusing each other of error and insulting each other with highly labored prose. This competitive spirit asserts itself in the variety of liberation movements. A Manhattan liberal wears the crown: he is working for the liberation of all persons imprisoned for political, racial, or religious reasons anywhere in the world. Although much of the pursuit of these causes is harmless, some of the activity, such as that of international causes, creates an impact out of proportion to the number of liberals participating in it.

Major political, social, and economic decisions in LME issue from liberal thinking. Even conservatives, once they acquire decision-making posts, are frequently nudged into liberal thinking as they enter the system; Republican fiscal responsibility becomes Keynesian economics once the advocates of fiscal responsibility acquire political office. Regardless of the label of those who make them, decisions tend to be the same when circumstances are similar. This style of decision making suggests in its evolution an over-reaction theory of social change in LME. To cite a hypothetical example: in stage one, liberals start beating the hustings over society's cruel treatment of homosexuals. They acquire support from high-minded politicians and from progressive organizations such as the American Civil Liberties Union and the National Organization for Women. A liberal law is passed. In stage two, the homosexuals reach such a level of daring that a man cannot move his bowels in a public rest room without being propositioned. Conservatives become indignant over this turn of events and in the next stage muster sufficient strength to pass another law. The law, under the vigorous leadership of the Federal Bureau of Investigation, places police guards at all public rest rooms. And on it goes to the next stage of police brutality and more reform. Social change generally runs along these lines, the net effect of which is overall movement toward an omnipotent state.

Liberals delight in platitudes. The specifics of a situation do not interest them. Thus, the liberal candidate for mayor of a large city declared during his campaign that the only solution to racial unrest was a community in which all races lived together in peace. He thereby placed himself solidly on the side of virtue. When someone in the audience suggested that integration could be achieved by limiting the influx of Blacks in white communities, he appeared shocked. He won the election to lead the city in a course of integration that runs from segregation to integration and back to segregation.

Liberals find employment in the upper echelons of the public bureaucracies in LME. In government they find a sanctuary from the rigors of

life outside. If their ideas of a better world cannot be brought to
fruition, government at least provides them a cloister away from the injustices of the larger society, and, in the upper echelons, a place to
apply their analytical frameworks on a global scale. In government, the
liberal formulates policy. In the educational system, he pushes it this
way and that with the latest fad. In industry, he provides the techniques with which to manage the consumer. One post is a springboard for
another. He moves together with his colleagues from one letterhead to
another as he marches from one cause to the next. The list used to run
from Roger Baldwin to Norman Thomas. Because of ravaging time and the
decline of the Wasps, the order now is Bernstein to Yarmolinsky.

In short, they are the standard bearers of ideas crystallized in
the Big Depression of more than four decades ago. Inside government,
they are prudent. Outside, they pronounce the truth and pour out books
that lament the errors of their predecessors in office. Their influence
does not derive from a mass following, although some are so deluded; it
comes, rather, from the princes of LME who pick and choose. When their
sway ends, there is always another set of liberals eager to take over.
If a Galbraith or a Schlesinger are disengaged and pouting, there is always a Brzezinski available. With some shopping around, a set of liberals can be found for every mood.

The liberal judges himself to be a humanitarian and man of universal
principle. However, consistency is not his virtue. The liberals who
find war barbaric would like to do some sabre rattling when it comes to
the Arabs. The horrors of war are more bearable when directed against
the bad guys. The liberal thus discriminates in his love for humanity;
he loves some people more than others. He has a sublime feeling for the
whole human race, but a special affection for black Rhodesians and South
Africans. He is disposed to abandon the use of intellect when a just
cause requires it. He shares with the society generally a penchant for
anti-intellectualism under pressure of self-interest, but he gives the
switch the name of justice. Justice for the liberal is what you get when
you get what you want.

His intellectuality blocks him from relating to one person at a time.
With a profound understanding of mankind, he finds it difficult to grasp
the character of any one person. He victimizes himself by stereotypes of
his own creation. Moreover, once a liberal assigns virtue to a particular
group, its members can do no wrong. He panders to their every impulse;
those who oppose are evil. Once a liberal makes up his mind, he loses his
liberalism. A person expressing a contrary view may be a demagogue, mis-
guided, or incompetent. Thus, in referring to liberals in the U. S. Congress who voted against busing of school children, Tom Wicker of The New
York Times writes:

> It was also, for those numerous liberals who knew
> better, rank demagoguery. Some others may only have
> been caught up in a stampede. Still others may have
> acted from genuine, if misplaced concern. All of them
> failed, in one way or another, to meet the ordinary
> standards of leadership and vision that ought to be ex-
> pected of members of Congress. 3.

Accordingly, the liberal embellishes phenomena in accordance with his
ideological outlook. The embellishment is sustained by selected facts
and so becomes a universal truth.

The liberal thus evidences characteristics of youth: a need to wor-
ship charismatic figures, confidence in one's own wisdom, and ignorance
of the subtleties of problems. The newspaper ad liberals who make their
pronouncements on issues suggest that the bitterest enemies of liberals
are other liberals. They denounce each other by exchanging letters.
They even state for the record how they denounced each other on the telephone.

The liberal's angel used to be the Negro. No matter how atrocious
the Black's behavior, it was understandable. The posture was tinged with
masochism. Some Blacks were not loathe to take advantage of the halo provided them. This posture provided the thrust to social policy whose economic and social costs the society continues to reap. The posture of virtue slaying evil inhibits upward communication. Fighting for equality,
liberals reap a harvest of divisiveness and separatism. They even incur
the contempt of the Blacks they used to champion. When the Kerner Commission on the Negro riots in the 1960's trumpeted its finding that white
racism was to blame, liberals reacted with enthusiasm. They took the
global conclusions to their bosom in a spirit of _mea culpa_, assuaged their
sense of guilt, and thereby alienated the white ethnics who traditionally
supported liberal causes. If LME cannot reform itself, the reason to a
considerable degree lies in this historical choice.

Liberals pontificate in the city about tolerance and then go home to
their suburban dwellings, while white ethnics whom they exhort to be fair
minded go to bed afraid in the city. Liberals push educational opportunities for Blacks while ethnics undergo heavy sacrifices to get one child
through college without the same subsidies. More out of vexation than the
merit of the position of persons they champion, liberals flit from the
white working class, to African Blacks, to Soviet Jews. The liberal politicians who seek justice for the Israelis are not unmindful of the fact
that there is a greater proportion of Jewish to Arab votes in their constituencies. The pursuit of interests is given a mantle of high morality.

---

3. The New York Times, November 9, 1971.

Similarly, the position of middle-class Blacks reflects their needs more than those of the black underclass. They share with white liberals a disclination to see things as they are.

Power fascinates. Liberal intellectuals, denied power, pout. They become critical of those who acquire it. They are not against the use of organized power so much as the manner and condition of its employment. By being critical of its use, they compensate for their inability to gain it. A sumptuous lunch in the ornate private dining room of a prince in LME is enough to give a liberal intellectual a sense of euphoria; aware of this weakness, industry and government take advantage of it. They hire intellectuals to perform tasks and are interested not in the end product of their toil so much as in the aura of respectability given their dealings. Undoubtedly, some of these employers may have a genuine interest in his product; undoubtedly also, some consider the intellectual a naive person who can be used for not fully disclosed purposes.

The social fabric that holds together society is a delicate one. Issues have to be resolved in a precarious nexus formerly held together by a national government symbolizing justice. That symbol has been severely damaged. Americans are less generous with each other, less inclined to make concessions to different points of view. They are disinclined to listen to what is in conflict with their views. They commit cruelty in the name of fair play. Uncommitted, they maintain a troubled silence. The intellectuals' mission of social betterment has failed to stem this tide. Where they exert some influence--in the university-- the intellectuals have provided a harvest of child-men.

The American intellectual does not convey the image of a man of culture. A more typical portrait is that of an insecure, humorless egoist, aristocratic in outlook, using shock to gain attention, lacking courage to concede mistakes, unable to talk man to man with persons outside his class, incapable of offering a substitute for the traditional philosophy he assisted in destroying. His cleverness does not extend to creating an alternative, not even for his own salvation. He is trapped in a life of futility, searching for gurus. He has destroyed his image as a man of learning. He is too impressed with the foolishness of lesser men. He does not affirm life. If by some biological coup, everybody became an intellectual, we would likely achieve a kingdom of abuse. In short, few intellectuals exist in the ranks of so-called intellectuals. History gave them the chance to lead an accommodation of social goals, but they blew it with their ego trippping. The non-intellectuals, so-called, have relegated the intellectuals to the trash can.

PART FOUR: It Will All Be Mafia

Chapter 10

How It Will All End Up

A revolutionary change in decision making has taken place in the American economy. The political-economic system of countervailing power has blossomed into an oligarchy of conservative managers of interconnected advocacies. They exchange positions periodically in a game of musical chairs. They are all-purpose heroes. A manager may be an executive in industry today; a top official in the military establishment tomorrow; the day after, a battler against world poverty in an international organization. The corporate lawyer who advises his firm one day on how to promote its interests with government may be a cabinet officer the next defending the public trough against corporate incursions. No major movement occurs in any one direction. However, a trickle of talent moves from firms and government to foundations and universities in order to pursue a sublime mission before retirement; there managers perform as elder statesmen and purveyors of truth after the rough-house and deception of industry and government. Thus, roving managers discharge the burden of administering LME through the management of money, property, skills, and connections. They operate in a climate of moral and esthetic insensitivity. They use the methods of the traditional mafia. The modern world is a mafia world.

To sum up the arguments that support this assertion, I must first restate the mafia principle and those social forces that underscore its validity. The mafia principle affirms that modern society abhors differences and narrows them by a process of leveling down and leveling up. From this distaste for differences, political forces emerge that, through public policy, seek to reduce disparities in income, power, and prestige. If persons fail to attain these goals, it is argued that such a result is the fault of society. Moreover, since nobody is responsible, everybody tends to be irresponsible. The logic of transferring culpability to the society assumes that it must be the duty of the state to reduce the dissimilarities. Liberal thought underwrites such a sublime mission.

-141-

The scenario leading to this style of welfare state first unfolds as society's members organize to pursue various rackets with which to reach the dominant goals of the society. The practice of seeking an exclusive racket to promote one's interests is not confined to the illegitimate mafia. With the passage of time, to acquire more cost effectiveness, the _mafiosi_ in the legitimate and illegitimate mafia adopt each other's methods. This exchange makes the norms of behavior of each subeconomy indistinguishable. Such practices as bribery, violence, merchandising, and monopoly control become universal. The methods of a Ford Motor Company become indistinguishable from those of a crime syndicate. Corruption--the disparity between actual and stated purpose--becomes more evenly balanced between the society's two components. The mafia mentality that pervades the society triggers events that lead to an equality of mediocrity under state tutelage.

Disaffected groups arise spontaneously either to pursue these dominant goals of the society or to protect what they have from the predatory actions of others. To minimize the possibility of backlash, each group prudently adopts procedures that fall within a gray area where notions of respectability and unrespectability commingle. For some groups, such as Italian-American crooks, this means leveling up. The sons of these men of affairs, for example, may go to Harvard Business School. For others, such as Wasps, this means leveling down. As practices become uniform, the disparities in corruption narrow.

By this irreversible drive toward equality, the suffering members of the illegitimate mafia achieve a moral victory. The new society becomes a testimonial to the worthy contributions that go back to the Sicilian pioneers. A bland sort of organized crime becomes universal. Indeed, since members of the same Italian tribe who migrated to Canada and South America did not organize crime syndicates, the force of logic commands this conclusion: the real _mafiosi_ are Wasps.

As the society gropes for this lowest common denominator, a mass man emerges whose vulgarity becomes chic. This mass man resents distinction and seeks to suppress it through political intervention. The upsetting effects of differences in intelligence, affluence, and influence compel the use of law to eliminate dissimilarities and to exert pressure to make them an improper subject of public discourse. The common man not only enjoys his coarse qualities but by means of the law imposes his values on others. To a considerable degree, the intelligent in LME's public and corporate life cater to the mass man in order to acquire prestige and income.

The suppression of differences cuts across the broad spectrum of public life: in college education it can be seen in the rise in grades as aptitude declines; in equal opportunity law; in commercial

television; in the political process where the politician must demonstrate that he is everyman; in the dissemination of public information; and in the hazards attending the performance of research that
suggests men are not equal. The person of distinction makes people
uncomfortable. He is a threat. He must be cut down and made to feel
unexceptional.

Accordingly, we live in an age of mass marketing psychology and
vanishing artfulness. Art, a vital component of the good life, has
become a spectator sport. The individual is controlled as a producer
and consumer in accordance with a mass plan calculated to achieve maximum returns. The decline of a cultural elite that shaped the society's
values, the emergence of a morality of permissiveness, the decline in
artful experience in the daily conduct of life, has given free rein to
the psychology of mass marketing.

This maximizing principle produces a search for a common denominator by which institutions increasingly adopt the methods of the traditional mafia. The principle is implemented in our major institutions.
The critical ingredient of these institutions is organization to pursue
self interest. The immediate consequence of organizations pursuing their
respective common denominator is homogenization of the individual. The
long-term result of this homogenization is a society whose members are
equal in outlook and social behavior, and whose tendencies toward any
inequality are corrected by an overseeing state.

The evidence of such evolution lies in the decline in the differences between the collective personality described by a computer and
the characteristics of an American selected at random. The state provides and the collective personality feels no pain in the lack of individuality. The mass media make a powerful contribution to this leveling up and leveling down. Television's role is particularly a formidable one. To note, for example, that a prominent person in the community also suffers from hemorrhoids is comforting. Indeed, of all the
society's major institutions, the mass media reveal the greatest mafia-
like tendencies. It is the only powerful institution in society that
demands, and obtains, the right to operate by its own rules.

From the axiom of equality one can deduce the subaxiom of no-
fault. The individual cannot be held responsible for the consequences of his choices when these choices are circumscribed by the behavior of other people past and present. It follows therefore that
the individual condition stems from deficiencies in the state's discharge of its obligations. Foremost among these duties is relief of
the citizen from an entrapment not of his own doing.

This no-faultism is irresistible as a movement. The politicians
who espouse it acquire more votes than those who don't. No-faultism

lies behind the slogan of equal rights and rationalizes confiscating the
fruits of productivity from the most culpable--the well-to-do--to give
to the least culpable--the less than well-to-do. The state guarantees
equality in return for submission to its bureaucratic vise. No-faultism
sanctions the pursuit of interests without regard for individual responsibility. The less than equal are relieved of responsibility.

In part, no-faultism is a reaction to the mafia syndrome in LME.
A predominance of Wasps in its high administrative posts suggests that
political connections rather than individual ability are a major criterion
of advancement. The unsystem reacts to this nepotism by imposing on LME
the ethic of no-fault. Moreover, the discriminatory responses of the
liberal press to this contemporary philosophy encourage no-fault. For
example, The New York Times, to redress society's wrongdoing, supports
a policy of state-administered racism in support of Blacks. But the same
newspaper looks with abhorrence at the way white ethnics seek to acquire
political advantage through bloc voting in order to promote their interests. A consequence of this inconsistency is no-faultism.

In economic terms, the push for equality represents a claim on
the productivity of others. Those who are not equal seek through political maneuvering to claim the product of others. The alternative--
raising their own productivity--is distasteful. The exercise of political power to equalize living standards entraps the more productive.
If they were to cease working with the intent of frustrating the efforts
of the egalitarians, enterprising politicians would place new claims on
their wealth. The search for equality is relentless so long as envy
shapes public policy.

Some organized efforts to promote equality are actually disguised
subsidies advancing the interests of particular groups over others. For
instance, many feminists demand equal rights to act like the bastards men
are. But they aspire to do so through a preferential quota system euphe-
.mistically labeled "affirmative action." However, this feminism is not
without its price within female ranks. Some women advance their careers
at the expense of sisterhood. The decline in sisterhood affords increasing similarity with the precarious status of brotherhood. The same preferential treatment is accorded Blacks. These efforts to acquire a competitive advantage generate a drive toward a quota system for all groups
in society in the pursuit of equality.

The goal of equality even lowers discrimination in the distribution
of heavenly rewards. Sin, fundamentally, is not a function of individual
proclivity but of opportunity. The greater presence of women in heaven
is due to their being denied equal rights to temptation. The state is
busily correcting this disparity.

These policies inevitably generate white male backlash. It is suggested that equity demands the door of sexism swing both ways. Thus, if the term "chairman" is offensive, parity requires changing the sign on the cage of the circus tiger from man-eater to person-eater. Accordingly, the abhorrence of differences generates a new consciousness. In a suit brought against a major city for alleged discrimination against women by its police department, the supporting evidence included a gun design that makes it difficult for women to grasp the trigger, a rule allowing women to carry handbags only during their menstrual periods, and the use of male-only police dogs. At Penn State University, the sexist Alma Mater song used to proclaim: "Thou didst mold us, dear old State, into men, into men." The words have been changed to: "Thou didst mold us, dear old State, dear old State, dear old State. The sexist term "alma mater" raises what appear to be insurmountable difficulties. A suggestion has come forward to discard the term for "alma mafater" and "alma famater", alternating between the two every six months.

The Equal Employment Opportunity Commission is faced with equally perplexing and relevant questions on equality. One can envisage the day when the commission will have to confront such matters as what percentage of ancestry must be black to be black; whether an Italian who changes his name to Gonzalez is thereby entitled to part of the Spanish surname quota; whether the EEOC should consider a petition of discrimination against women by a male who undergoes sex surgery; or whether an artificial insemination laboratory can reject a sperm donor applicant solely on the basis of sex.

This movement toward equality is physical as well as social in character. As the hernia rate for the working classes declines, the ulcer rate for the system's managers rises. As workers increase their leisure time, the governing class spends more time (with increasing futility) at its posts. Managers and managed breathe the same polluted air. Violence, once confined to working class districts, spreads to the fashionable areas of the city. As the lung cancer rate for women rises, another inequality fades away. Girls drink and become drunk as often as boys. He becomes more like she, and she like he.

So why fight the inexorable? Should we not nudge these leveling forces along and urge the mafia principle as smoothly as possible to its logical result? Some public policy suggestions come to mind. We could reduce social distinctions through organized sports. Games could be put together at the initiative of the White House between members of the system and those of the unsystem. A baseball game between teams captained by the board chairman of the Gulf Corporation and a mafioso operating a chain of brothels could clear the air. Second, we could develop a technology whereby the people can alert LME's managers to their aberrations from state norms. A device emitting a Bronx cheer could perform such a task. The White House in particular should be connected to such a circuit. As an additional measure, the demands of college students for courses more relevant to their experience could be realized in sociology electives including Applied Vulgarity, Black Sociology, Protestology, and Do-It-Yourself Explosives Engineering. The fertile minds of sociologists in developing relevant courses should be used to advantage. Additionally, the conflict fostered by value differences might yield to enterprising solutions. For example, the practice of teaching girls to combine sex with affection and boys to catch-as-catch-can poses a problem in social engineering. The demand for accommodating girls exceeding the supply could be met by a government financed social program under liberal sponsorship. Additionally, to extend the practice of racketeering, instruction could be provided to the public early in the careers of students. Not the least important component of such instruction would be techniques in exploiting fear, ignorance, and fantasy. For such teaching, visiting professors from television and advertising would be useful.

The affirmative action policies of equal opportunity law suggest possibilities for the narrowing of differences. The percentage quota for Blacks could be extended to white ethnics. Top managerial posts could be reshuffled to reflect the nation's ethnic composition. The President of the United States might want to approach the Arab members of the oil cartel and try to make a deal in exchange for a generous quota for Arab-Americans. The Wasps, Hessians, and Jews thus displaced by Americans of Polish, Slovak, and Italian stock could be resettled in the unsystem. Is there a better way to break the grip of the illegitimate mafia? Is there a better way to raise the degree of equality in mankind--or should I say--personkind?

Here and there one sees evidence of increasing equality for women. The entrepreneurial talents traditionally reserved to men are appearing in women. For example, one woman has come up with the fantastic idea of stimulating interest among adopted children to trace their genetic origins. The plan has endless possibilities for increasing the gross national product. Almost everybody acquires the urge at some point in life to search for one's true self. The greater difficulty this inquiry has for adoptees would generate greater expenditures and thus have an accelerator effect on the GNP. The income of psychiatrists would increase geometrically as each adoptee initiates a campaign in search of roots. The successful tracking down of biological parents would trigger the need for psychiatric assistance for four persons and possibly five, including the adoptee. Her organization, ALMA (meaning soul in Spanish) and an acronym for Adoptees Liberty Movement Association) has chosen as its motto: An adoptee's ignorance of his true origins may lead to his or her serious malfunctioning. From such examples, there is every reason to believe that the racketeering propensity of American males can be developed--through supporting legislation if necessary--in women.

B. F. Skinner proposes an imaginative technique to rid the American public of the burden of taxation through an extension of the lottery and to produce thereby an equality in good feeling. An important resource, he points out, has been neglected--the schools--and the behavioral technology is at hand to employ them. Skinner proposes a system of lotteries extending from kindergarten through high school in which the odds are at first highly favorable to bettors but grow steadily worse until, upon graduation, the student will find the standard lottery with its meager odds irresistible. Within twelve years, the schools of the nation would be graduating dedicated gamblers. Within a few years thereafter, it will be possible to abolish state sales and income taxes and subsequently property taxes. The abolition of even federal taxes would follow. In a brilliant stroke of conditioning by the system, the people feel free and happy. 1.

The twentieth century began in an atmosphere of hope that scientific reasoning would produce a high moral order. It seems destined, as the century closes, to go down as an era in which the major contribution of such thinking was charlatanism and manipulation. Scientism's promised age of splendor has materialized as one of control. Like the Greeks, the managers began to feel that the knowledge acquired by the few is ineffective if left to the discretion of the less wise. Political action, therefore, should encourage people to behave according to a plan. If the individual demurs from accepting what is good for him, he has to be manipulated. The ideal form of such control is one in which people behave in pre-programmed fashion but believe they are exercising their free will.

So, in the future society of the twenty-first century, the forces that confirm the mafia principle's truth will finally triumph. By the end of this century, the policies of government and corporation will have at last obliterated differences among the people. Distinction will have disappeared. The normal having absorbed the increasingly accepted abnormal, the distinction between normality and abnormality vanishes. Liberals will have exhausted opportunities to pursue worthy causes; they will lose interest after tracking down the grandchildren of Nazi criminals and passing legislation forbidding the transmittal of Nazi genes. The corporations, media, and government will win their battle of inducing the people to prefer fantasy over reality. Fantasy and not reality will command authority. Only the chief of state and his retinue of mandarins will be privy to information describing reality. A selected number of these mandarins will be catapulted into space laboratories for periodic refurbishing, including organ transplants. The descendants of the old-fashioned mafiosi will become civil servants operating the gambling empires of the state. Violence will be taken over by government and corporations to become more sophisticated and uniform. Typical forms will include electronic eavesdropping, illegal plugging into computer systems, and surreptitious polluting.

---

1. B. F. Skinner. The New York Times, July 26, 1977.

Accordingly, after decades of noisy demands for human rights--a euphemism for claiming other people's income--the people acquired all sorts of rights from the state and with them lost their freedom. But they did not grieve over their loss. An infantile bondage toward their politicians gave them economic security. A policy of equality in employment, education, and leisure liberated the people of any sense of inferiority. Society's most heinous crime became any expression of difference in outlook, attire, and behavior. Pushed upward into the bureaucratic structures by the policy of equal opportunity, functional illiterates with undergraduate college degrees first created a crisis in management. The problem was resolved by converting the new managers into the attendants of machines controlled by the mind machine of the chief of state. The people were plugged into the first level of machines. In the next order were the scientists and engineers, and in the last, the chief of state with his circle of mandarins.

How did this perfect society arise? With the assistance of the mass media, the public became organized, directed, and represented in accord with the technology of conditioned response developed from the crude beginnings in advertising. Because of the threat to equality generated by free thought, the society fostered mindlessness in production and leisure. The only permissible discernment was reserved for the capo, the chief of state, plugged into the mind machine during his or her term of office and fed information by eunuch scientists and engineers. Removed from the machine upon expiration of term in office, the capo rejoined the ranks of the mindless. He/she lowbrows with vestigial organs roamed the earth. Sexual activity was managed by government in accord with cost-benefit calculations performed by the universities. The feminist movement persuaded men that their greater aggressiveness had social and not biological foundations. So persuaded, with the help of drugs, men became more docile.

To promote efficient governance, the people were piled high in a few metropolitan areas along the polluted coasts, managed by invisible and inaccessible bureaucracies. Thousands of toilers manned (and womaned) posts .at fortifications designed to forestall any tidal wave throwing back pollution into the people's faces. Occasionally, the capo appeared on television, an image of the average man/woman, exhorting the populace to perform deeds in the interest of greater equality. To direct the public will, sub-chiefs in the government and state corporations employed merchandising techniques developed by professors from university conglomerates. The traditional three branches of government--the legislature, the executive, and the judiciary--exercised total control over the lives of the citizens. From time to time, the Supreme Court announced ex cathedra the new morality, including the conditions under which fetuses, babies, and adults should live. The collapse of the lower courts attending the rise in litigation over equality generated a need for judicial decisions rendered by administrative fiat without rights of appeal. The collapse became imminent by 1984 when the Equal Employment Opportunity Commission had accumulated a ten-year backlog

of Blacks demanding their rights and when criminals, coming in and out of
the judicial system between periods of rehabilitation at hideaway resorts,
brought the system to a standstill. Public officials moved into public
places enshrouded in plastic bubbles reaching below the genital organs to
the interest of national and personal security. The number of high-level
bureaucrats who succeeded in getting positions of power to compensate for
their character flaws was reduced by mandatory psychiatric examinations
for high-level positions.

The acute food shortage attending the right of the world's poor for
equality forced the passage of a law prohibiting Americans from eating in
other than communal kitchens of the state. In keeping with the policy of
government support of private enterprise, the communal kitchens were operated under government contracts by a collegium of fast food organizations
including McDonalds, Ginos, and Burger King. After extensive lobbying in
the U.S. Congress, the collegium succeeded in forcing the passage of legislation imposing stiff penalties for the surreptitious eating of hamburgers
in private homes.

Another law passed at the turn of the century was an amendment to the
Civil Rights Act of 1964 prohibiting the use of the terms "man" and "woman"
both in the singular and plural in gatherings of two or more individuals.
The minimum was raised to three after a fervent plea by Italian-American
Congressmen to allow heterosexual partners to use such terms in reference
to each other. The compromise was unsuccessfully attacked by liberal groups
as a throwback to the old days of romanticism. Moreover, Italian-Americans
were constantly giving trouble by persisting in their differences. They
produced few illegitimate births, stayed off the welfare rolls, did not de-
sert their families; they rarely divorced and looked upon government as an
instrument of evil. These aberrations created serious difficulties in the
march toward equality.

Another piece of social legislation forbade intra-ethnic marriages.
The law was triggered by an ethnic imbalance not caught by the computer.
Toward the end of the century,equal opportunity policy assigned quotas to
all ethnic groups in the society in accordance with their relative number
in the population. Initially, these quotas created disruptions. Wasps in
high government and corporate posts had to be re-settled in the ranks of
the old mafia. Because they exceeded their quota in university positions,
Jews, Indian Indians, and Chinese had to give up their jobs, and, in the
interest of ethnic balance, retrain as university maintenance personnel.
Matters appeared to settle down then the Italian-Americans created a crisis
by a surge in their fertility rate. Another liberal law was passed controlling fertility rates in order not to upset the ethnic balance.

There were many legal battles before the society achieved perfect
equality for all ethnic groups. As an example of the tenure of these
skirmishes, Italian-Americans succeeded in passing a law forbidding
the use of the vulgar Anglo-Saxon term for sexual intercourse as a:

noun following the word "mother". This unanticipated and deplorable state of
affairs hurt black ethnic pride. Black liberals retaliated with another
piece of legislation imposing penalties on the use of the same Anglo-Saxon
term as an adjective ending in the letters en. A new era of compromise
was ushered in through an amendment to the basic legislation of 1964
allowing the term's use as an adjective if the ending were ing.

Back in the late 1960's and some years thereafter, the myth had grown
in society that the young people were going to lead the population out of
the woods with their love and insight. A troubled homosexual had written
a best-seller to that effect, and his work had been heralded by many university liberals, including John Kenneth Galbraith. A sociologist, Theodore Roczak, was a prominent contributor to the myth. As it turned out,
by the end of the Indo-China War, it appeared that the love children were
actually frightened to death by the thought of being shot at and soon forgot
with the termination of the conflict what their assigned mission was. Undaunted, Roczak abandoned the love children and reassigned the sublime
mission to bearded gurus from the Far East. But the gurus did not succeed
in stopping the movement toward equality by conditioned response; they were
too preoccupied with managing rackets of their own in religion.

The nineteenth century liberal ethic of promoting the greatest good
for the greatest number, a morality that emerged in the twentieth century
as brain control and homogenization of people, reached its preeminence in
the twenty-first. The liberals acquired what they would not have dared
to think of obtaining in their wildest dreams; a no-fault society whose
members' needs were provided by the state. A dutiful population executed
the leveling policies designed by the machines of the managerial-scientific
caste. With the exception of the managers and scientists, the population
lost the ability to use language precisely. But this loss was in accord
with the purposes of the state. Ideas were conveyed through the flashing
of television pictures. The only needed response was a grunt indicating
receipt of message, or, in the case of non-receipt, an expression of black
English majors: wha' dat? As in ancient Inca society, the population was
assigned specific roles. The life of the individual--in consumption,
housing, entertainment, marriage--was under state supervision. The people
could not write, but the skill was not needed. A secret police force over-
saw their behavior. They supported a governing bureaucracy who granted
themselves the only special privileges tolerated in society. Like B. F.
Skinner's experimental pigeons, the population was imprinted to perform
mechanically in accordance with the best interests of the state. Only
the capo, plugged into a thinking machine guarded around the clock by
armies of the Secret Service, knew what was actually transpiring.

Life in the society of conditioned response equality comprised a
routine similar to the life of ants: a series of mechanical acts for the
good of the whole. The individual achieved a perfect adjustment to the
role assigned him by the state. In the absence of instability, tension,

and expectation, his (or her) emotions atrophied. In the absence of any further need for progress, there was no sense of going places. Equality became genetic as well as social in scope. Since physical distinctions would create tension, the differences were progressively eliminated through genetic engineering. Under a redefined meaning of equal opportunity, the individual acquired not only rights of education and employment but also equal rights of heritage. Modern technology and no-fault equality interacted to produce a mass man that did not have to experience the pain of learning, desire, or choice. He behaved as a collective personality, rewarded with a living standard not markedly different from that of anybody else. After a long history of discord and violence in the last days of the twentieth century, the people at long last settled down to a life of no pain, no emotion, and no judgment.

But then the zest for life began to ebb in the ensuing decades. The country gradually became a tomb. A digging anthropologist from a faraway nation, sifting through the remains of American civilization, unearthed information that the people had focused their lives on the veneration of equality.

Chapter 11

Synthesis

The capitalism that has emerged since the pre-industrial era of
Western culture is not the one anticipated by Marxist theory. Karl
Marx foresaw an inexorable march in accordance with scientific law
toward liberation of the working class by means of a collective control of society under the beneficent hand of government. What Marx
failed to foresee is that the mass man emerging from capitalism is
inclined to trade his sense of inequity and his involvement in the
affairs of society for economic security and amusement. Marxist
theory is a powerful explanatory tool that went astray by its pre-
diction of a revolution against capitalism followed by a dictator-
ship of the proletariat.

Instead, a society of organized advocacies has emerged that seeks
to control the perceptions and values of a passive citizenry. The decline in participation by the electorate goes on relentlessly. At the
same time, with the support of government and the mass media, the producer corporate advocacies develop and manipulate values as a means of
controlling public expenditures. The alternate school---television---
instructs the child several years before the traditional school. Once
they begin to compete for attention, each system acquires about the
same amount of time. The public school system primes the educational
pump of television by its atmosphere of permissiveness in ideas and so
prepares children for matriculation into the school of television.
And when these children become adults, many of them rely exclusively
on television for their source of information. Thus, organization at
one stage in the evolution of capitalism serves the individual and then
in the following seeks to adapt the individual to serve the organization.

Accordingly, to say that values arise from the method of production,
as the Marxist thesis states, is an over-simplification. The relationship between values and production technique may have been valid in a

simpler world when production was confined mostly to life essentials.
However, as more and more of production has come to involve goods and
services that people have to be instructed to want, the values inculca-
ted by producer advocacies through the mass media have overrun any that
might have arisen from the method of production. Moreover, in the artificial environment in which urban man finds himself, he has become an
easy prey for the propaganda ploys of the organized advocacies including
government.

What people prefer, and the way they relate to each other and to
the society, now depends upon the varying success with which organized
advocacies, principally those of the producer variety, inculcate values
in the interest of maintaining organizational needs. With the able aid
of the mass media, the producer advocacies have replaced folk culture
with a vulgar culture designed for profit. The crowd asserts its right
to this vulgarity and to impose it on others.

What keeps the fragments of this social process together is control
by big organizations of their respective constituencies, and, in conflicts of interest between them, by an accommodation either directly or
through the intervention of government. The government does not solve
problems so much as it periodically redistributes their burden in accordance with the political power of the organized advocacies, including producers, income recipients, and critics of the system.

The crowd does not participate. It is a spectator. The crowd toler-
ates control because it is often not conscious of such control, and because it acquires in exchange economic security and amusement. And the
managers of organized advocacies have been eminently successful in persuading the mass that their goods and services provide the means to well-
being and happiness. Additionally, this success in control is enhanced
as the crowd deludes itself into believing it has freedom. It is only
when the crowd's freedom of movement is curtailed that it becomes enraged.
Marx's tenet of alienation brought forward the belief that the worker
feels powerless because of his exclusion from the decision making process. Today's modern employee, to the contrary, does not care about such
involvement provided he is given the opportunity to consume, to be amused,
and to be managed with a light hand by his bosses.

When these comforts are threatened, the recourse of the crowd is not
to responsible participation but to disruption. Moreover, its sense of
outrage is often directed against the innocent. For example, the new public employee class(which was supposed to be in Marxist theory the instrument for emancipation of the working class) pursues its own interest at
public expense. While blue collar workers in the private sector continue

to play by the rules, the public servant has become the public master. The new public class has no compunction about inconveniencing the public it is supposed to serve. This insensitivity to the needs of the community as a whole has produced a collapse in the sense of commonweal. Each organized advocacy seeks its full pound of flesh subject only to the restraints that can be imposed by other advocacies.

Thus, the posture of the new capitalism of organized advocacies is, on the one hand, big organization inculcating values for the maintenance of its prestige, income, and power, and, on the other, a homogenized mass that seeks equality in security and amusement. The classes in the traditional Marxist sense have all but disappeared. The workers themselves are divided. The new drama is one of control by the managers of organized advocacies and containment of the undesired effects of control when matters go awry. The media, not only in their development of mass tastes, but also in their fixing of the political agenda and candidates for office are an important source of control.

Moreover, the energies of the system are essentially political in character. Its posture, its information dissemination, its value formation, and its judgments are based on political calculations. The truth is whatever smart politics convinces the public is the truth. Deception is right; being caught at it is wrong. The ethical standard is: if it succeeds it is all right. Problem solving is not an act of rational analysis, although at times it pretends to be, but an exercise of politics in which those with the greater influence have the greater logic.

This contest of power is sharpened by attorneys who hone positions of advocacy at the expense of accommodating the sense of fairness. The explosion of litigation is undermining the sense of mutual trust. It cannot be arrested through legislative relief because attorneys control the legislatures.

What are the outcomes of such a system of organized advocacies? First, its corruption is inevitable because the managers of resources mistrust and therefore do not fully reveal their intentions to the crowd. The crowd, not altogether undiscerning, senses this inclination and so the relationship between both becomes one of mutual mistrust. Moreover, there is not only a corruption of purpose, but, in order to maximize acceptance, a corruption in any given response. Second, the operant values are not those that serve individual growth, but those that serve the needs of organization. This politicizing of values is even reflected in judicial opinions that dispense justice based on the points of view of those in political ascendancy. Third, it often comes to pass that the policies promoted by organized advocacies are often opposed by a majority of the electorate.

Accordingly, the evolution of western society is not liberation of the individual but his control by big organization in exchange for economic security and titillation. And this control fosters an equality of mediocrity. The combat for resources between organized advocacies precludes the possibility of pursuing a vision of excellence. Additionally, to the spectator person, any suggestion that he is inferior in any way is intolerable. And the advocacies take this posture into their calculations. Each group reaches for a common denominator that would maximize its constituency. The pressure of each group is relentless so long as other groups appear to fare better. Greed and insensitivity feed the combat. The struggle continues so long as differences in income, prestige, and power exist among them. Each group seeks either the support or the acquiescence of the crowd, or failing both, tries to neutralize its influence.

At times, the advocacies combine with other advocacies to acquire more control of a particular area of interests. Or the big may swallow the little. To maintain their vigilance, they give money to legislators and hover over the legislatures like a vulture circling over its prey. Their information is inherently corrupt; it is not designed to enlighten, but to assemble facts in a manner that promotes vested interests. And their propaganda is likely to become more effective as computers speed up their barrage of information and as their political action committees legalized recently by the Supreme Court acquire additional resources.

This effect of advocacies excluding the individual from control is found also within the folds of government. For example, the military combine, while living on public money, has succeeded in eliminating the citizen as an instrument of control. Complex military technology provides the rationale for setting aside democratic accountability and making choice a private affair. The individual has neither the money nor the technical information with which to lobby side-by-side with the military lobbies.

Moreover, the advocacies can obstruct effective solutions to problems. Each major problem triggers intervention and lasts until adoption of the solution. Even the media, by their sensationalism, by their oversimplification, and by their intrusion into the news play no small part in the process of weakening solutions.

Two systems of justice exist in a society of organized advocacies: one for the isolated individual and another for the advocacies manipulating the legislatures and the judicial system. The individual in difficulty is unable to command effective resources against advocacies. By contrast, the corporations that violate the law in the amount of billions of dollars annually do so with impunity. Corporate crime gets no more than a slap on the wrist for several reasons. The attorneys who defend the corporation are more competent than those in the government administering the law. The corporation, moreover, can muster considerable resources in its defense and finds it advantageous to drag on litigation endlessly in such areas as labor relations, pollution, antitrust, tax evasion, bribery, and fraud. It pays to litigate rather than to assume social obligations. Last, the government overseers of the corporation often have similar ideologies and are reluctant to bite the hand that may some day feed them.

In this system or organized advocacies, the individual vanishes. The selfsame liberal advocacies that claim to promote individual rights make a formidable contribution to the creation of the homogenized person. In the name of promoting his interests, the individual is being reduced to a homogenized entity. If he wishes to avoid such a fate, he must seek influence through a group. But by so doing, he becomes a political creature and loses his individuality anyway. Such has become the legacy of liberalism.

We live in an age where the price of adulthood is judged to be in excess of its benefits. It is an age in which the children of hedonism demur from assuming the responsibilities of adulthood. Like children, we are given to a dependency on exteriors to titillate and comfort us; an abhorrence to reality; a preference for fantasy over discernment, and security over the taking of risks; an unwillingness to wait for long term gains; an inability to sustain expression; a penchant for rage if we do not get our way.

This age has been labeled in different ways: the technocratic society, the post-industrial era, the narcissistic society. Each label provides insight by observing events from a different dimension. But the many forces on the stage refuse to be capsulated by three words. If one were reaching for the era's attitude of mind, the age of infantilism would be no less appropriate.